The Transport for London
Puzzle Book

The Transport for London
Puzzle Book

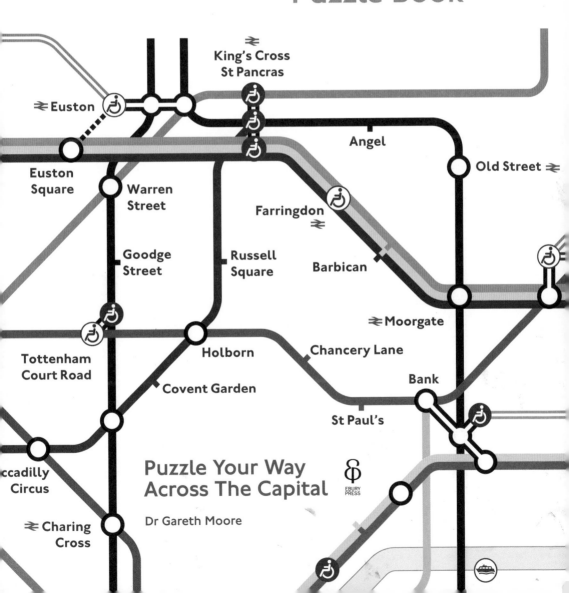

Puzzle Your Way
Across The Capital

Dr Gareth Moore

I

Ebury Press, an imprint of Ebury Publishing,
20 Vauxhall Bridge Road,
London, SW1V 2SA

Ebury Press is part of the Penguin Random House group of companies whose
addresses can be found at global.penguinrandomhouse.com

First published by Ebury Press in 2020

www.penguin.co.uk

A CIP catalogue record for this book is available from the British Library

Design created by Amazing15
Design and layout by Tom Cabot/ketchup
Text by Dr Gareth Moore
Project management by whitefox

ISBN: 9781529106343

Images on pp. 150–151 © Shutterstock
Mapping on pp. 138–139 © Crown copyright/Ordnance Survey (OS)

Printed and bound in China by C&C Offset Printing Co., Ltd

Penguin Random House is committed to a sustainable future for
our business, our readers and our planet. This book is made from
Forest Stewardship Council® certified paper.

⊖ Contents

Introduction

Whether you've lived in London for years, are an occasional visitor or have never been here at all, it's time to test your knowledge of both current and historical London transport with this book of puzzles that is as varied and as interesting as the story of transport in London itself.

Transport for London (TfL) was built on historical foundations that date back to the 19th century when the world's first underground railway, the Metropolitan Railway, opened between Paddington and Farringdon in 1863. Since then the Underground network, affectionately nicknamed the Tube by generations of Londoners, has grown to 270 stations and 250 miles of track, with 11 lines stretching deep into the Capital's suburbs and beyond. The development of London into a pre-eminent world city during the 19th, 20th and 21st centuries would not have been possible without the mobility provided by the Underground, and later by TfL's extended network of buses, trams, riverboats, the Overground, DLR and more.

TfL's iconic roundel design, developed first for the Underground but later applied across London's transport network, has permeated pop culture and become a firm fixture in literature, film and art for over a century. Indeed, most Londoners have an emotional connection to the vast transport system that threads its way through the capital's neighbourhoods, hearts and minds.

The puzzles in this book cover the rich heritage of TfL, including challenges based on everything from classic Underground posters through to the history of stations and services across London. If you're an expert on the Tube map – or London transport history in general – then you'll be in heaven, but even if you aren't then all of the puzzles have been designed to be approachable for almost any reader.

There's a Tube map on the back inside cover of the book, although if you're familiar with the map already then I suggest trying to solve as much as you can without resorting to checking it. The puzzles are also jam-packed with trivia throughout, so no matter how much – or little – you know about TfL and London transport in general when you first pick up the book, you'll be something of an expert by the time you complete the final challenge.

The book is broken down into five chapters, each covering a different type of puzzle – although inevitably there is some overlap between topics. The first two chapters are dedicated to word puzzles, of a wide range of types, with the second chapter particularly focusing on cryptic and code-based puzzles.

In the third chapter, you'll encounter a wide range of maps and map fragments, as well as historical roundels, posters and even moquettes – the iconic fabric patterns used on the various TfL transport services. The fourth chapter contains a huge variety of grid-based puzzles, all themed around transport, and then the final chapter covers a broad selection of trivia-based questions, all presented in interesting and novel ways. Even if you don't know much about London transport, you'll still be able to make headway with many of the questions in here.

It's worth noting that all of the content can be read in any order, so there's no need to work through page-by-page – unless you would like to, of course. Full solutions are at the back, and often they have further information or explanatory text to an answer – so they're well worth checking, even if you are sure of the answer.

I hope you have as much fun puzzling through this book as we had writing it!

Dr Gareth Moore, May 2020

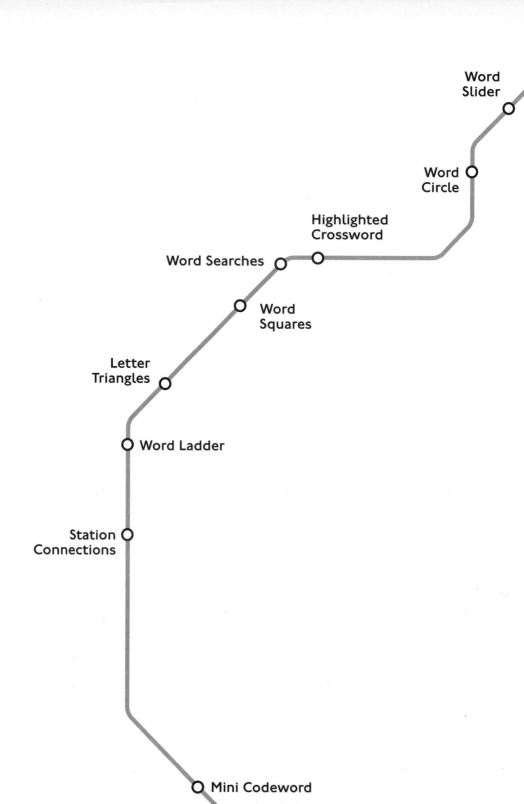

Word
Slider

Word
Circle

Highlighted
Crossword

Word Searches

Word
Squares

Letter
Triangles

Word Ladder

Station
Connections

Mini Codeword

WORD PUZZLES

Mini Codewords

In these puzzles, all of the letters spelling out the names of **TfL stations** have been replaced with numbers. Can you work out which number has been assigned to each letter in order to reveal the hidden stations? No two letters are represented by the same number, nor vice versa. Use the table beneath each puzzle to keep track of your deductions.

1. The following six stations all begin with the same letter as a London Underground line that serves them. Hint: Two of the stations both have the same second word. What could that second word be?

6	9	13	13	10	13

I	7	2	4	4	7

3	9	5	4	13	12	9	16

4	9	I	7

16	10	10	2	5	9	7	4

6	12	9	13	6	4	2	8

11	9	13	4

14	9	15	17	12	9	11	11

18	9	19	4	2

I	7	2	4	4	7

1	2	3	4	5	6	7	8	9	10	11	12	13	14	15	16	17	18	19

Single-station Close-ups 1.

Can you identify the unlabelled station based on just the colours of the Underground lines shown?

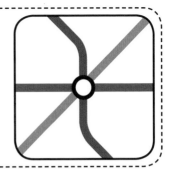

2. The following six stations can all be found on the London Overground. Hint: This journey travels anti-clockwise.

7	3	9	13	1	5

10	4	13	3

11	3	13	15

2	10	18	6	20	15	18	9

4	6	20	3	10	4	1	5

11	8	1	10	12

20	3	14	7	8	1	6

10	17	3

14	1	9	18	9	2	16	10	17

14	1	6	19	3	9

10	18	1	19

1	2	3	4	5	6	7	8	9	10	11	12	13	14	15	16	17	18	19	20

3. The following six stations can all be found on the Docklands Light Railway.
   Hint: This journey travels from west to east, skipping some stations.

7	12	12

15	7	2	8	14	15

1	7	15	14

2	8	11	2	7

4	10	17	7	12

5	2	13	14	10	4	2	7

13	17	3	4	9	15

6	7	12	12	2	10	8	15

4	1	7	13	19

16	1	13	18	14	10	8

1	2	3	4	5	6	7	8	9	10	11	12	13	14	15	16	17	18	19

Letter Soup

Five words relating to tickets and fares have been scrambled together to make a soup of floating letters. Can you unscramble the letters to re-assemble the original words? Each floating letter is used exactly once.

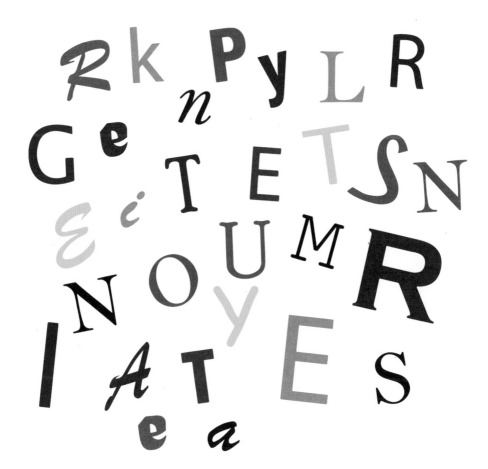

Station Connections

1. Write one letter per box below to form a list of six stations that can be visited, in the order given, by travelling on the London Underground Victoria line in a single unbroken ride. The lines between boxes mark **all** places where successive station names share identical letters, as well as selected other connections.

   Hint: this journey travels north to south.

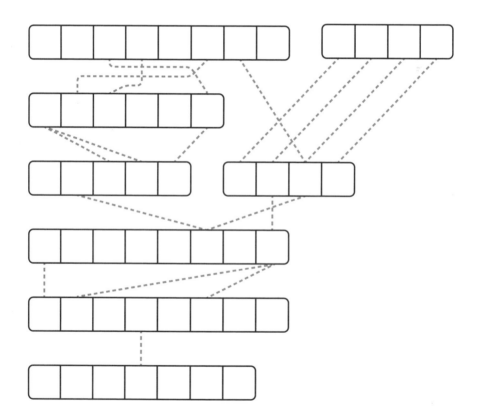

2. Write one letter per box below to form a list of six London Underground terminals. The lines between boxes mark **all** places where successive station names share identical letters. The terminals are not in any particular order.

Hint: Try starting with the final station in this set, due to its length.

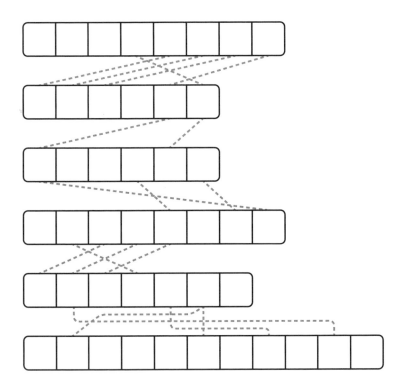

Station Connections

3. Write one letter per box below to form a list of Underground stations that can all be found **on or within the bounds of the Circle line** (as drawn on the standard map).

Unlike the previous two Station Connections puzzles, only **some of** the letters which are shared between successive station names have been labelled.

Hint: Three stations have pairs of letters linked in their second word. What could these second words be?

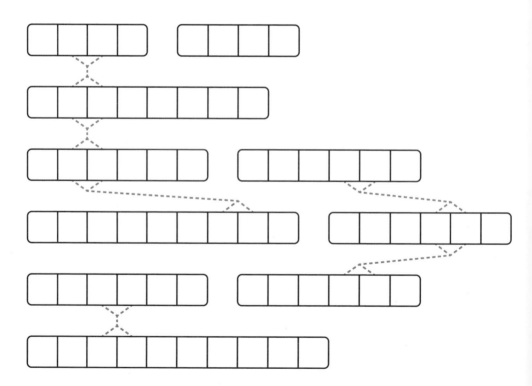

4. Write one letter per box below to form a list of stations that can all be found on the London Underground Map. As in the puzzle opposite, only **some** of the letters shared by successive station names have been marked – but those given are sufficient to uniquely fill the puzzle.

Hint: Note that all the stations start with the same letter, and try looking for the two longest station names first.

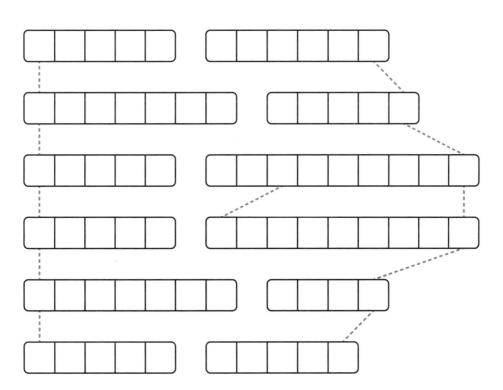

Word Ladders

Can you travel from one station to the other along each word ladder? Fill in the top and bottom slots by completing the names of two London Underground stations, then travel by changing one letter at a time to create a new four-letter word. Letters can't be rearranged.

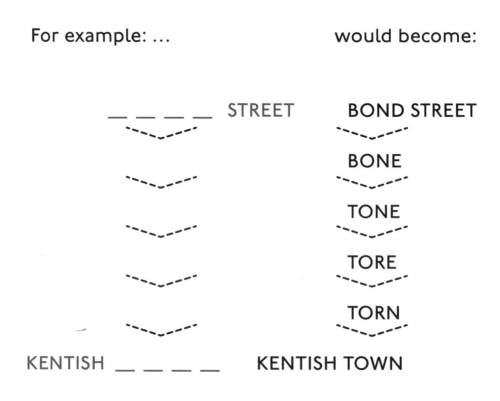

For example: ...   would become:

_ _ _ _ STREET   **BOND STREET**

                                    BONE

                                    TONE

                                    TORE

                                    TORN

KENTISH _ _ _ _   **KENTISH TOWN**

1. COLLIERS <u>W</u> <u>o</u> <u>o</u> <u>d</u>

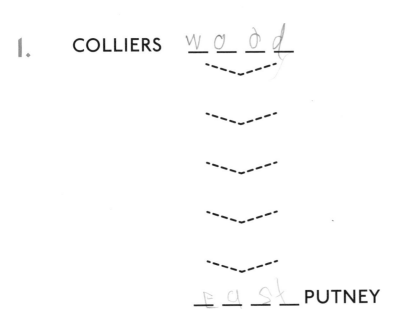

<u>E</u> <u>a</u> <u>st</u> PUTNEY

Bonus Question: How would you travel on the Underground from one station to the other with only one change of train?

2. CHALK <u>F</u> <u>a</u> <u>r</u> <u>m</u>

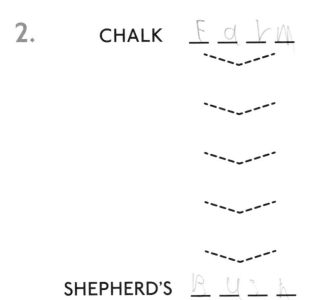

SHEPHERD'S <u>B</u> <u>u</u> <u>s</u> <u>h</u>

Bonus Question: Both of these stations are in the same fare zone. Which zone is it?

3. In the following ladder, the first station has no clues. Given that all the words required in the chain have four letters, what is the first station?

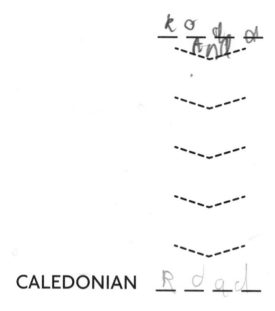

CALEDONIAN _R_ _o_ _a_ _d_

Bonus Question: There are only two London Underground stations with four-letter names. One appears in the ladder above, but which is the other one?

Bank oval

Letter Triangles

Can you place all of the lettered triangles into the shaded block so that they spell out a phrase you might hear while standing on a station platform? The phrase, when read from left to right, top to bottom, is made up of five words – although spaces have not been included in this puzzle.

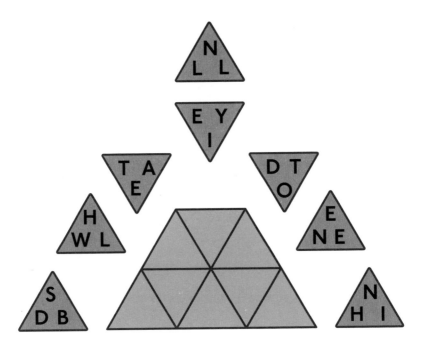

Word Squares

Can you find the clued words hidden in the squares on these pages by tracing out a path from letter to touching letter, without visiting any letter more than once? You may travel diagonally between letters.

The final clue for each square uses every letter.

1.
a. The colour used for the Central line
b. A cardinal direction
c. _____ Lane, DLR station
d. Major London venue, the O2 _____
e. The official sponsor of the London bicycle hire scheme since 2015

D	N	A
E	N	T
R	A	S

2.
a. Something some people do at The Oval
b. Emirates _____ line, TfL cable car
c. It's required to row on the Thames
d. If you travel by way of somewhere, you travel ___ there
e. A suitable vehicle for exploring the Thames

T	R	E
B	A	V
O	R	I

3.

a. Complete the phrase:
   'Full speed _____'

b. Predicted time a vehicle
   will reach its destination
   (3-letter abbreviation)

c. The average interval
   between trains or buses
   on a regular service;
   progress

d. Typically British hot drink

e. District line station in zone
   5 (two words)

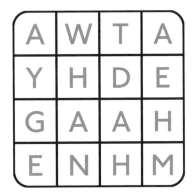

4.

a. _____-a-Ride, TfL door-to-
   door service for disabled
   passengers

b. Travelling from place to
   place, _____ about

c. Fee for using a road, bridge
   or tunnel

d. Name of a now-demolished
   tower in the Tower of
   London

e. London Tram station east
   of Croydon (two words)

5. This final word square conceals the name of a certain type of more occasional TfL transport. To make it easier to find, no diagonal moves are required to reveal it.

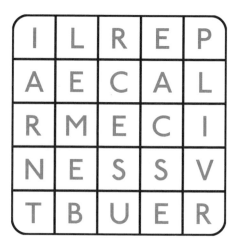

I	L	R	E	P
A	E	C	A	L
R	M	E	C	I
N	E	S	S	V
T	B	U	E	R

Single-station Close-ups 2.

Can you identify the unlabelled station based on just the colours of the Underground lines shown?

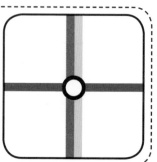

Notting Hill Gate

Codeword

Crack the code to reveal a completed crossword grid, where every horizontal and vertical entry is an ordinary English word. The four highlighted words are transport-related terms, and the circled letters spell out an anagram of a two-word station on the Underground. Some letters are given to get you started.

Use the letters down the sides of the grid, and the table beneath, to keep track of your deductions.

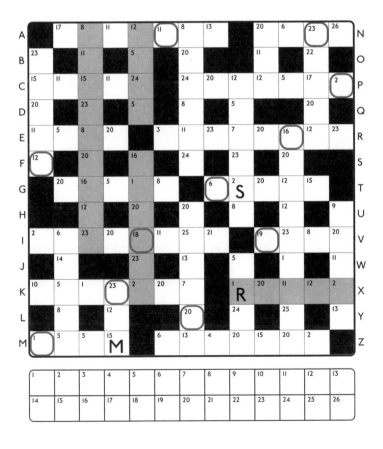

Word Search: Finding Your Way

Can you find all of the TfL stations in the word search grid? Words may be written in any direction, including diagonally and backwards. Every compass point in a name, however, has been replaced with a compass symbol in the grid.

ALDGATE EAST
CLAPHAM NORTH
DAGENHAM EAST
EAST HAM
EAST PUTNEY
EASTCOTE
HOUNSLOW WEST
LAMBETH NORTH
MILL HILL EAST
NORTH ACTON
NORTH EALING
NORTH GREENWICH
NORTH HARROW
NORTH WEMBLEY
NORTHOLT
NORTHWICK PARK
SOUTH KENTON
SOUTH RUISLIP
SOUTH WIMBLEDON
SOUTH WOODFORD
SOUTHFIELDS
SOUTHGATE
SOUTHWARK
WEST BROMPTON
WEST FINCHLEY
WEST KENSINGTON
WESTBOURNE PARK
WESTMINSTER

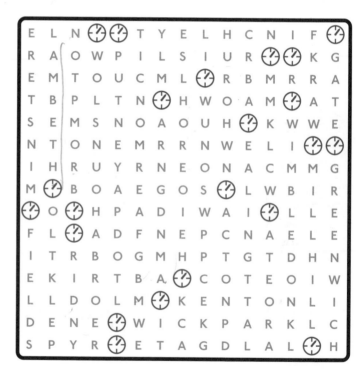

Word Search: Missing the Bus

Can you find all of the bus stop names in the word search grid? Words may be written in any direction, including diagonally and backwards. The centre of the grid is missing, so you must complete it as you fill the grid in order to be able to place all of the bus stops.

ABBEY ROAD
ALDGATE
ALDWYCH
BAKER STREET
BANK
BOND STREET
CAMDEN ROAD
CAMDEN TOWN
EDGWARE ROAD
ESSEX ROAD
EUSTON
FLEET STREET
KING'S CROSS
LISSON GROVE
MARBLE ARCH
MARYLEBONE
PADDINGTON
PARK LANE
QUEENSWAY
ST PAUL'S
TOWER HILL
VICTORIA
WESTMINSTER

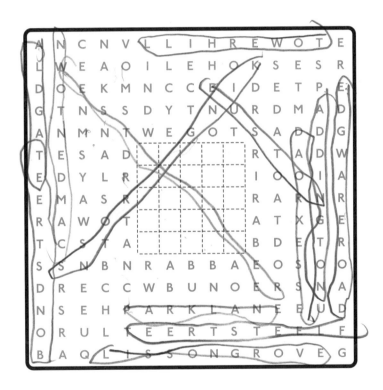

Highlighted Crossword

Can you complete the following crossword, using only transport and TfL-related words? Once you have finished, the highlighted squares will spell out an anagram of a related name.

ACROSS

1   Sightseer (7)
5   Vehicle with overhead cables (4)
6   Advertisement display (6)
8   Place to embark or disembark (7)
11 A double-decker, for example (3)
13 Capital of England (6)
14 Fare payment card (6)
15 Space between train and platform (3)

DOWN

1   Informal term for the Underground (4)
2   Somewhere to sit (4)
3   Navigation tool (3)
4   Short stay for 1 across (5)
7   Form of TfL's logo (7)
9   Ceramic wall coverings (5)
10 Underground railway passage (6)
12 Place to get on or off transport (4)

Word Circles

Each of these circles conceals a range of words, all of which can be spelled by taking the centre letter plus two or more of the other letters (but without using a letter more than once per answer). Solve the clues to reveal six or seven from each circle.

1.

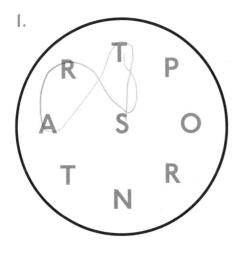

a) This relevant word uses all of the letters in the circle

b) Complete the DLR station name:
star LANE

c) Something to hold onto on the Tube

d) Which 'Office' operated their own London underground railway until 2003?

e) Places ships sail from

f) It sounds like he might be found at a 'Green' Underground station on a green line

a) Find two station names that end in 'Street': _Bond_ STREET; _Aldey_ STREET

b) Complete the station name:
MILE _End_

c) Former name of The O2 Centre: The Millennium _Dome_

d) Travel indirectly to a specific location, as a river might do

e) Complete the phrase: '_Mind_ the Gap'

f) This station uses all of the letters in the circle

2.

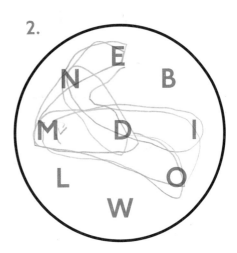

Tube-line Crossword

Fill the crossword below with the names of TfL stations, ignoring any spaces. The numbered clues show you which line, or lines, serve each station, so for example a green dot would indicate the District line. They also show you the length of each word in the name of the station.

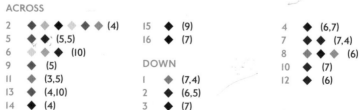

ACROSS

2 ◆ ◆ ◆ ◆ ◆ ◆ (4)
5 ◆ ◆ (5,5)
6 ◆ ◆ ◆ (10)
9 ◆ (5)
11 ◆ (3,5)
13 ◆ (4,10)
14 ◆ (4)

15 ◆ (9)
16 ◆ (7)

DOWN

1 ◆ (7,4)
2 ◆ (6,5)
3 ◆ (7)

4 ◆ (6,7)
7 ◆ ◆ (7,4)
8 ◆ ◆ ◆ (6)
10 ◆ (7)
12 ◆ (6)

Zig-Zags

1. Complete this puzzle by writing a letter in each space given so that every row contains the name of a London Underground station. The final two letters of each station name then become the first two letters of the following station, as shown. Each station is a single word long.

CARPENDERS 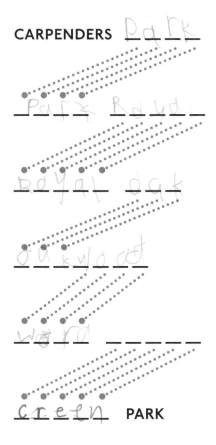 Park

Park Road

Royal Oak

Oakwood

Wood _ _ _ _ _

Green PARK

ARSEN al

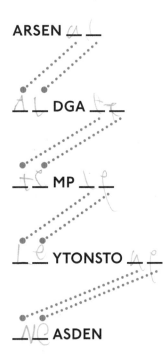

al DGA te

te MP le

le YTONSTO ne

ne ASDEN

2. Complete this puzzle in a similar way, but using the names of six London Underground and Overground stations. The final word or letters of each station name becomes the start of the next station, as shown.

Poster Fitword

Fit all the unobscured words of two or more letters shown on the poster below – advertising the brand-new Tube map of 1908 – into the empty crossword grid. Any words which appear more than once in the poster appear a single time in the grid, and punctuation has been ignored.

To make it trickier, the grid has been rotated randomly so you may need to turn the book before you start to fill the grid.

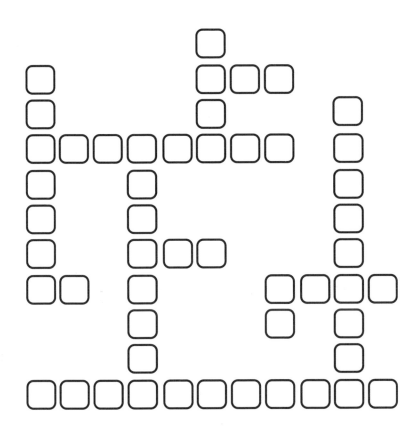

Single-station Close-ups 3.

Can you identify the unlabelled station
based on just the colours of the
Underground lines shown?

Green Park

Common Terminals

Make each of the following words into the name of a TfL station by adding the same suffix to both words in each pair. All of the suffixes are words in their own right, and every station name will be a single word long.

1. GUNNERS
   QUEENS

2. KEN
   PADDING

3. FIELD
   ARCH

4. WEST
   UP

5. WOOD
   GREEN

Single-station Close-ups 4.

Can you identify the unlabelled station based on just the colours of the Underground lines shown?

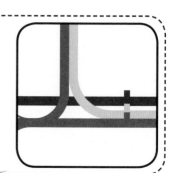

Gloucester Road

Word Slider

By sliding each of the vertical strips up and down, how many of the words clued below can you reveal in the window? As an example, 'BACK' is currently readable.

1. Tube station interlinked with Monument
2. Most commonly occurring word in Tube station names
3. Designer of the first iconic Tube maps, Harry _____
4. Former name for London Trams – the Croydon Tram _____
5. London Transport's first Chief Executive, Frank _____

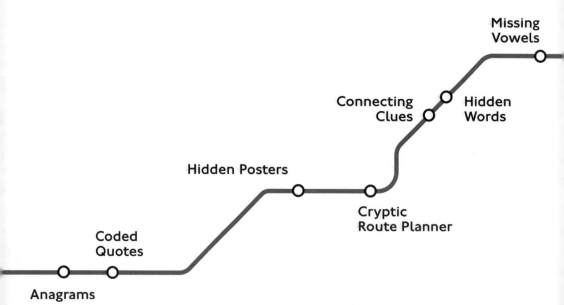

Missing
Vowels

Connecting
Clues

Hidden
Words

Hidden Posters

Cryptic
Route Planner

Coded
Quotes

Anagrams

CODE &
CRYPTIC PUZZLES

Anagrams

The words below are all anagrams of **stations which have interchanges served by three or more Tube lines**. Can you unscramble the letters and reveal the names of these busy stations? Spaces and punctuation may differ to those in the station name.

1. IDLE MEN

2. WORE A LOT

3. DOG AND PINT

4. WRITTEN MESS

5. LOVELIEST REPORT

6. LATE TO LIGHTNING

7. TOUGHNESS IN KNOT

8. TOP GARDENER TARTLETS

Poetic Anagram Extras

Each line of the poem below forms an anagram of a **station on the London Overground**, plus one leftover letter. The leftover letters, when read in order from top to bottom, reveal the name of another London Overground station. Spaces and punctuation in the anagrams may differ to those in the station names.

1. TREE-CUTTER SKY, _____

2. SLEEK AS RAIN. _____

3. KNEW DANGERS <u>Kew Gardens</u>

4. ON THE MOOR: _____

5. WET PATH MADNESS. _____

6. HEALTH, WET BRAIN! _____

7. A RAW AND ACUTE _____

8. HELL, DRAWS _____

9. A LEADEN HONESTY. _____

Coded Quotes

TRAVEL QUOTES

The following quotes related to travel have all been encrypted using a Caesar shift. Each letter has been substituted with another a fixed distance along the alphabet, so with a shift of I then A would become B, B would become C, and so on, until Z became A.

Each phrase has been encrypted with a different shift, although the same shift is used for every letter within each phrase. Can you work out the shifts and reveal the quotes?

1. Tkbkx mu ut zxovy cozn gteutk eua ju tuz rubk
   – Kxtkyz Nksotmcge

2. Wkh zruog lv d errn, dqg wkrvh zkr gr qrw
   wudyho uhdg rqob d sdjh – Vdlqw Dxjxvwlqh

3. T eclgpw qzc eclgpw'd dlvp – Czmpce Wzftd
   Depgpydzy

4. Vwb itt bpwam epw eivlmz izm twab –
   R. Z. Z. Bwtsmqv

5. Qoxsbi fp cxqxi ql mobgrafzb, yfdlqov, xka
   kxoolt-jfkabakbpp – Jxoh Qtxfk

LONDON QUOTES

Two well-known quotes about London are given below, but all of their words have been listed in alphabetical order. Can you rearrange the words to restore the two original quotes – and then can you discover who they are each attributed to?

A	IS	MAN
A	IS	OF
BIRD	IS	OF
EVERY	LIFE	ROOST
FOR	LONDON	TIRED
HE	LONDON	TIRED
	WHEN	

Single-station Close-ups 5.

Can you identify the unlabelled station based on just the colours of the Underground lines shown?

Hidden Posters

The top of the text on each of these two posters has been obscured. Can you use your skill and judgement to work out what each poster originally said?

Poems on the Underground: Anagram Endings

The last one or two words of each line of this poem have been anagrammed to form one or two new words (although the number of words in the anagram does not necessarily match the number of words in the original text). The anagrammed text is indicated in italics. Can you untangle the anagrams and reveal the original poem?

'TAGUS, FAREWELL' BY SIR THOMAS WYATT

Tagus, farewell, that westward, with thy *masters*,
Turns up the grains of gold already *tired*,
With spur and sail for I go seek the *ham set*,
Gainward the sun that show'th her wealthy *riped*,
And to the town which Brutus sought by *dear Ms*,
Like bended moon doth lend her *dusty isle*.
My King, my Country, alone for whom *I veil*,
Of mighty love the wings for this *I've gem*.

Poems on the Underground: Finish the Verse

The words which make up each line of the final verse of this poem have been arranged into alphabetical order. Can you rearrange them to restore the verse?

'BALLAD OF THE LONDONER' BY JAMES ELROY FLECKER

Evening falls on the smoky walls,
   And the railings drip with rain,
And I will cross the old river
   To see my girl again.

The great and solemn-gliding tram,
   Love's still-mysterious car,
Has many a light of gold and white,
   And a single dark red star.

a a garden I in know street

_____

ever knew no one which

_____

a beyond I know rose Thames the

_____

and are few flowers pale where

_____

Cryptic Route Planner

1. Can you use these cryptic clues to trace a journey across the Underground network?

   Hint: There's a full Tube map on the inside cover of this book.

   - Start at a station whose name features two colours, on a line with a compass point in its name

   - Travel south, past a place to mine bright white rock, until you reach a rabbit's home road

   - Take the monarch's line to a verdant recreation ground, and hop onto the line a shade darker

   - Travel past the armoured soldier's crossing to the first quadrangle you reach of an aristocrat, then change to a line the same colour as found in the names of two stations you've already visited

   - Travel south through a wide thoroughfare with a sliced meat in its name. Continue over the Thames, and on to the line's terminal

   - What might you watch here, if the weather is kind?

2. Can you also trace this second cryptic journey? This time you'll need to use the London Overground too.

- ◆ Tap in at what sounds like an overpass of the same colour as the line which serves it, then travel south to a station sharing a name with Shakespeare's birthplace

- ◆ Leave the Underground and travel west, changing trains at two interchange stations who share the first part of their name with a type of carriage, and continue south-west to the end of the line

- ◆ Change to a subterranean line which is not in reality the shape it claims to be, and travel anticlockwise until you reach the dedicated toolmaker, without changing trains

- ◆ Take a short stroll to change to a line with at least five terminals, then travel east to a queen

- ◆ Take the queen's line until you reach a station where a queen's angry husband is found alongside a holy person

- ◆ Change to the line that opens with the French underground, and travel east until you reach a station you have already used as an interchange

- ◆ Where are you, and what do you notice about the order of the colours of the lines you have taken on your journey?

Two Words, One Word

Eight one-word TfL stations have each been split into two regular English words. For example, **Warwick** could have been split into **war** and **wick**. From the clues below, can you decipher which two words are being individually described, and then combine them to reveal the station names?

1. Natural harbours + liquid

2. Monarch + rock from side to side

3. Citrus fruit + dwelling

4. Earth + slide

5. Applaud + unit of weight

6. On-hand supplies + water source

7. Heath + type of entrance

8. Snowy + chantry

Link Words

For each pair of words shown below, find a third word that can be added to the end of the left-hand word, and the start of the right-hand word, to form two new words. The number of letters in each of these 'linking' third words is shown. For example:

GRID _ _ _ _ SMITH would be solved by LOCK, to form GRIDLOCK and LOCKSMITH.

All of the missing words have a transport theme.

RAIL	_ _ _	SIDE
SIDE	_ _ _ _ _ _	LIST
IN	_ _ _ _	BLOCK
BATTLE	_ _ _	BY
TRAM	_ _ _	NATION
VAN	_ _ _ _ _	ANT

Connecting Clues

For each puzzle, start by identifying the five or six TfL stops or stations described by the clues. Once you have done that, can you work out the transport connection between each set of stations? Each set uses a different mode of transport.

1.
a. A place to keep your savings safe

b. An elongated circle

c. A heavenly being

d. A curved entrance support

e. A solid barrier to prevent flooding

f. Site of a famous Napoleonic battle

Connection:

_____

2.
a. A tall tree

b. Company founded in 1600: ___ ___ Trading Company

c. A Mediterranean island

d. The first Windsor monarch

e. An album by the Beatles

f. Celebrated London concert venue: ___ ___ Hall

Connection:

_____

3.
a. The home of the muffin man, according to rhyme

b. Site of Nelson's vertiginous monument

c. A famous statue of Eros resides here

d. Name of a flat horse race that sounds like a source of acorns

e. Duffy's 2008 single set in Little Venice

Connection:

_____

Single-station Close-ups 6.

Can you identify the unlabelled station based on just the colours of the Underground lines shown?

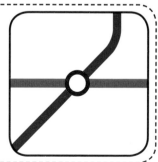

Aldborn

Hidden Words

Can you find the name of a TfL station hidden in each of the following sentences? In each case, the name of a service passing through the station is given to help you.

Example:
Don't worry about the Oyster card, Barb, I can pick it up when I next travel in on the Circle line. (solution: Barbican)

1. Charles, Dennis and Simon all took the Bakerloo line to Charing Cross.

2. 'Stop the bus!', he yelled, when he realized he'd gone past the stop for the Overground.

3. Always take care when stepping from the Central line onto the platform.

4. If you need to report a lost or stolen item, please contact a member of District line staff.

5. Victoria helpfully offered to sit alongside us to navigate the journey more smoothly.

Initials Only

The following classic works of literature set in London have been disguised so that only the initials of each title and its author remain. Can you complete the rest of each word and restore the names of the masterpieces?

G E by C D

M D by V W

T A O S H by A C D

T P O D G by O W

S C O D J A M H by R L S

Merged Stations

In this puzzle, the names of two Underground stations found on the same line have been mixed together, taking one letter in turn from each name. For example, BANK and OVAL merged together would give BVNL (B from Bank, V from oVal, N from baNk and L from ovaL), or alternatively OAAK.

Can you separate the merged stations and reveal their original names? To help you, the names have been shaded in the same colour as the Tube line which serves them. Spaces are correct.

OAFRRN CTREUT

PARSOOS HRUEE

SORTTWORD

SAECHSRES GUTH

PADYIEGOOE

KMNAIKGEOT

Letter Pairs

1. The following London Underground lines have been disguised by adding in extra letters. Can you delete one letter from each pair in order to reveal the hidden lines?

DB IA SK ME RT RL OL LO

CN IO NR BT HK LE RA LN

VJ UI TB IR LO AE TE

PM EI ET RD BO PA OC CL IC TL AE LN

BC IE KN OT RT IA NL

DC IE SR LT IR IC CE LT

2. The following names of vehicles used by TfL – both current and historical – have been disguised in the same way. Delete one letter from each pair to reveal the hidden vehicle models. You will need to insert a space into some of the answers.

RS OT LO CL IS NT GN SR TM OE CS KA

RT OR OU LB LT ER DY SB TU SR

GR EO UN TE ER ME DA FS TC EL KR

HF IA CG KE NM EO YB CG EA RE RT IO AT GA ET

VQ AU IR TI ON FB EA JH NE

RL OE YU LN AI NM BD TH IW TA LA NO

Every Other Letter Removed

1. The following London stations have each had every other letter removed to conceal their full names. Can you fill in the blanks and reveal the hidden stations?

LIVERPOOL STREET

BOND STREET

LEICESTER SQUARE

MARYLEBONE

KING'S CROSS

Bonus Question: What do these stations all have in common?

2. The following TfL-related words and phrases have each had alternate letters removed to conceal them. Can you fill in the blanks and reveal the hidden travel vocabulary?

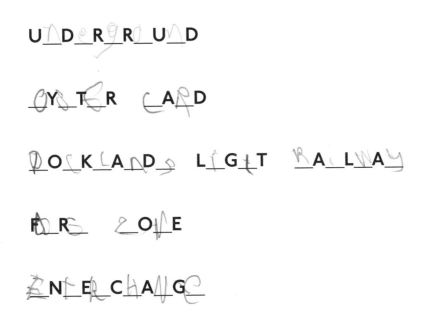

U_D_R_R_U_D

_Y_T_R _A_D

_O_K_A_D_ L_G_T _A_L_A_

_ R _O_E

_N_E_C_A_G_

Bonus question: Which of these was introduced in 1987?

Word Fragments

1. The following word fragments make up pieces of five London Underground station names that all have two double letters. Arrange the fragments in the correct order to restore the five station names. All of the stations are at least two words long.

ARE	CAN	COT	EN	EN
ET	GA	GE	GRE	HI
ING	LL	LL	LLE	NO
NON	RE	RUS	SD	SE
SQU	SS	ST	SWI	TA
TE	TT	WI		

2. The following word fragments can form five phrases from signage which can be found on the London Underground. Rearrange the fragments to restore the phrases.

AT	CE	FOR	GAP	GHT
IN	MA	MI	ND	ND
ON	ORI	OUT	PRI	RI
RVI	SE	SE	STA	THE
THE	TION	TY	WA	Y

Semaphore

A semaphore-style communication signalling system was in place on the London Underground for many years, through until 1953. Semaphore traditionally uses two flags, held up in distinctive positions, to spell out letters of the alphabet, as follows:

Using the guide opposite, decode the following slogans from TfL posters:

1.

2.

3.

4.

Coded Sets

1. The names of four **London Overground stations** are all encrypted in the same way in the text below. Can you crack the method of encryption and reveal them? Hint: There are four stations, and four letters in each group.

BSWW	EIAE	TLNS	HVST
NETB	ARER	LSAO	GTDM
RRPP	EEAT	EERO	NTKN

2. The names of five **disused London Underground stations** have all been encrypted in the same way below. Can you uncover the method of encryption and then restore their original names? Hint: All the letters you need are given – but they have been rearranged in a certain way.

ADRO ONPTOMBR

ETREST WNDO

WNTO SHTIENH KUTSO

MEUUSH MISITBR

TEETRM SIALLWI NGKI

Missing Vowels

1. All of the vowels and spaces have been deleted from the names of the **London bus terminals** below. Some extra spaces have also been added in to disguise the original names. Can you restore the vowels and original spacing to uncover the terminal names?

LD WYCH
D GWR
STN
XBR DG
RP NGT N
WLL SDN BSG RG

2. Each of the **TfL properties** shown in the left column below has been modified in the same way, by deleting vowels and altering spacings. Reveal the original words and then match them to the corresponding description on the right. Every TfL property and description must be used in exactly one pair.

K W D	Tube line and station
C VN TG RDN	Overground transport
LN D NT RMS	Tube station
MBN KMNT	Tube station and home of the London Transport Museum
RL LNGS TCK	Railway vehicle
R TMS TR	London Riverboat pier
VC TR	Bus model

Visual Stations

Can you work out the names of the London Underground stations represented by the following images?

For example:

would be Elephant and Castle.

1.

2.

3. _waterloo_

4.

finsburypark

5. KEN ----→  I TON _kennington_

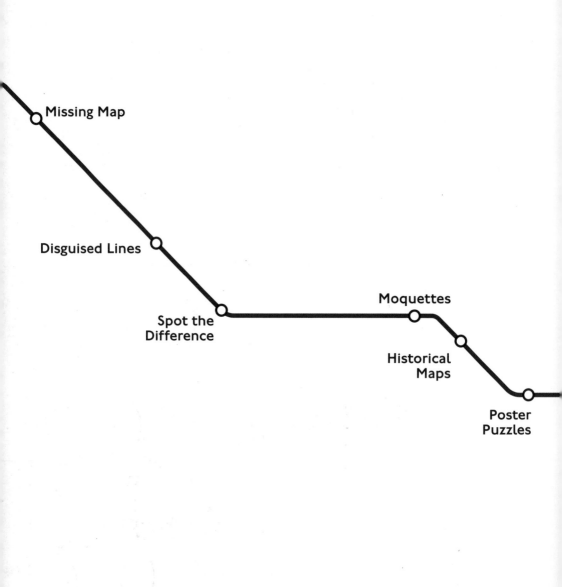

Missing Map

Disguised Lines

Spot the
Difference

Moquettes

Historical
Maps

Poster
Puzzles

VISUAL PUZZLES

Missing Map

Can you identify each of the stations shown on the map close-ups below, all of which have had their names removed? Most of the maps also have additional questions, which may in some cases help you to identify some of the missing station names.

1. Can you name the stations labelled A to I in this close-up?

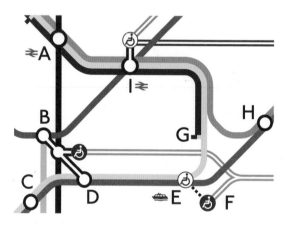

A. _Moorgate_
B. _Bank_
C. _Cannon street_
D. _Monument_
E. _Tower Hill_
F. _Tower Gateway_
G. _Algate_
H. _Algate East_
I. _liverpool Street_

♦ Which two of the stations shown were linked in 1933?
♦ Which of the stations was the original terminal of the Central line?

2. Can you name the station in this close-up?

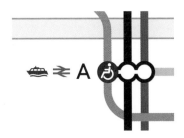

A.
Waterloo

3. Can you name the station in this close-up?

A.
kings cross st pancras

4. Can you name the stations in this close-up? The two stations have the same name despite being considered distinct stations, served by different lines.

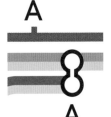

A.
Edgware road

◆ Both stations are named after the road which occupies the route of a former Roman road. What was the name of the Roman road?

5. Can you name the stations labelled A to D in this close-up?

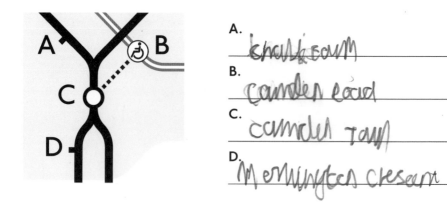

A.

ShalkFarm

B.

camden eoud

C.

camden Tawn

D.

Mornington cresent

◆ Which one of the Underground stations shown here was originally proposed to have the same name as the Overground station shown?

6. Can you name the stations labelled A to E in this close-up?

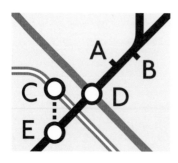

A.

oval

B.

Kennington

C.

Clapham Highstreet

D.

Stockwell

E.

Clapham North

◆ Which of these stations was the original terminal of the City & South London Railway in 1890?

◆ Which of the Underground stations shown has a track loop built in to reverse southbound trains and direct them northwards again?

7. Can you name the stations labelled A and B in this close-up?

A. _Wimbledon park_

B. _Wimbledon_

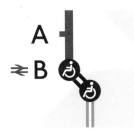

A

B

◆ In what year was the interchange station created to integrate the re-introduced tram service, Tramlink?

8. Can you name the stations labelled A to C in this close-up?

A. _Surrey quays_

B. _New Cross_

C. _New Cross Gate_

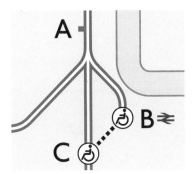

A

B

C

◆ Which one of these stations is named after the English county it used to sit on the boundary of – although it no longer does?

Disguised Lines

1. Can you identify the London Underground line shown below, taken from the Tube map? To disguise it, its distinguishing colour has been removed along with all of its station names and labels. It has also been rotated. Which line is it?

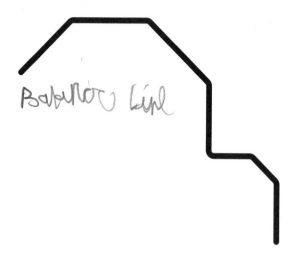

Bakerloo Line

Please note that these line graphics are taken from Tube map A (May 2019). Other versions of the map may not exactly match these drawings.

2. This line has been disguised in a similar way too. Can you identify it?

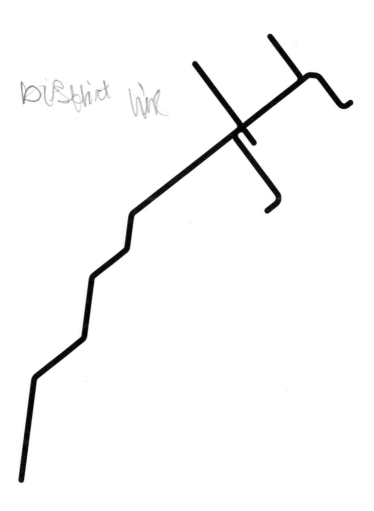

Spot the Difference

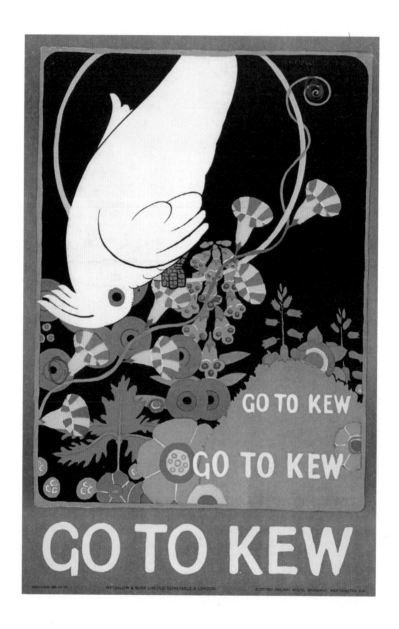

1. Can you spot five differences between these two images? The original poster, shown on the left, was designed by Maxwell Ashby Armfield in 1915.

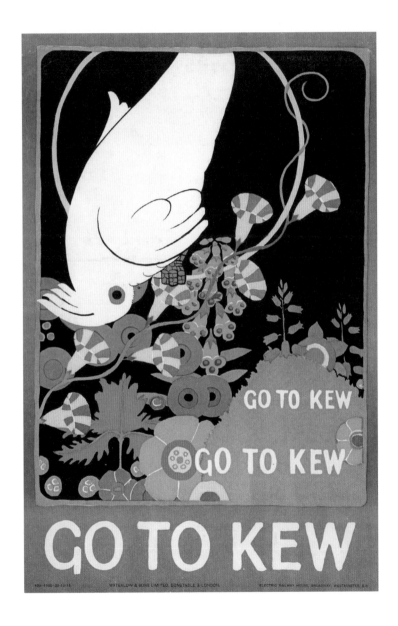

2. Can you spot ten differences between these two images? The original poster, shown on the left, was designed by Horace Taylor in 1924.

BRIGHTEST LONDON
IS BEST REACHED BY

Moquettes

Moquettes – the iconic and hard-wearing fabrics which cover the seats on TfL trains and vehicles – display great variety in their designs. Many of them conceal hints, often in the colours used, as to the line they are used on. Can you match each of the descriptions with a different one of the moquettes shown below?

1. This moquette is known as Barman and features four London landmarks in its design. It can be found on the Central, Northern and Jubilee lines.

2. This moquette was designed for the Green line fleet of buses, with contrasting colours in the pattern possibly representing the distinction between town and country.

3. This pattern also appeared on a fleet of buses, with this particular route using 'one-and-a-half' decker bus models and running a shuttle service between passenger check-in terminals and airport terminals in the 1950s.

4. This moquette – named 'Straub', for its designer – was commissioned for use on the first Victoria line trains. Due to time constraints another design was used instead, and this moquette entered service on a wide number of lines in the 1970s.

5. This moquette – named for the Tube line it featured on – features a design element which for many years was used on this line's iconography in place of the now-ubiquitous roundel.

6. This moquette was chosen for use on an Underground line after a public poll; the dazzling geometric pattern has been designed so that whole squares or rectangles could be cut out neatly in case of the need for small repairs to the fabric.

7. This pattern has never been used on a public transport vehicle – instead, it was designed specifically for use inside the cafe of the London Transport Museum.

8. Created by textile design duo Wallace Sewell – who also designed the Barman moquette, among others – this moquette is used on the London Overground services which first opened in various stages in the 2000s.

9. This moquette has been designed for the new Crossrail project which, when opened, will be known as the Elizabeth line.

Historical Maps

1925 MAP:

F. H. Stingemore

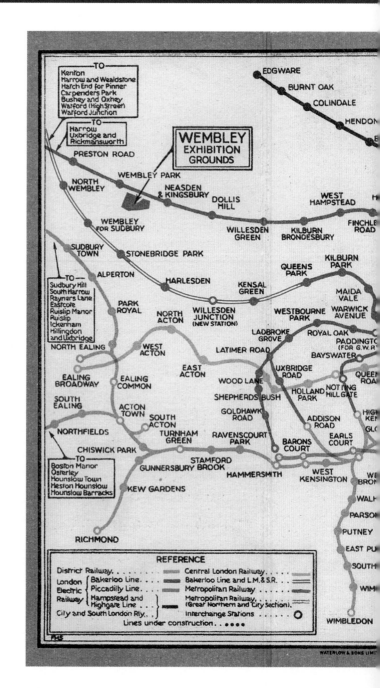

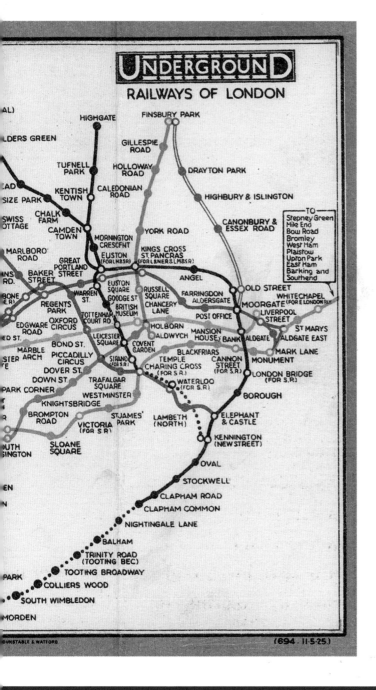

1925 Map: F. H. Stingemore

1. Can you find a station on the Central London Railway line serving – and named after – a major London attraction? The station has since closed.

2. In what way does the position of Mornington Crescent station differ from its representation on current TfL maps?

3. Which two railway lines shown on this map were eventually combined to form the Northern line?

4. What distinguishes the labels for Warren Street and Goodge Street stations from others on this map?

5. Two adjacent station names shown on the Piccadilly line – which share the same initials – no longer appear on the Tube map. What are they?

6. One of the two stations in the answer to the previous question is now closed. Which of the two stations is it, and what was its building temporarily used as after its closure in 1932?

7. The other station in the answer to question 5 has since been renamed. What is its current name?

8. What colour is used on modern TfL maps to represent the line shown on this map in orange? And what colour is now used to represent the line shown on this map in red?

9. Which major feature of London's geography is missing from this map, but included on modern Tube maps?

10. Which station shown as 'under construction' on this map is now known as Clapham South?

11. Non-interchange stations are shown on this map using filled-in circles in the same colour as the line passing through it. Without checking, can you say how they are represented on modern Tube maps?

1933 MAP: H. C. Beck

1933 Map: H. C. Beck

1. a. Which two stations on this map were replaced by a new station, which kept the name of one of them?
   b. Which modern line is that new station now served by?

2. What name is given on this map to the line now known as the Northern line?

3. Which station shown on the Central London line is now named St Paul's?

4. Which station on the Piccadilly line was renamed in 1932 having formerly been known as Gillespie Road? The new name appears on this map, but it has since lost the suffix shown here.

5. Which Underground line, opened in 1898 and running between only two stations, is not shown on this map despite being in operation when the map was printed? The line is still in operation today.

6. Several terminals for the District line are shown within the map area. How many of these are still District line terminals today? Note that one has since been renamed – and can you say to what?

7. Interchange stations are marked with diamonds, with each line involved in the interchange generally having its own diamond in the individual colour of the line.

   a. Which station on this map has the greatest number of such interchange diamonds?

   b. Without checking, can you say which shape is used to denote interchange stations on modern TfL maps?

   c. Again without checking, where can diamond shapes still be found on modern TfL maps?

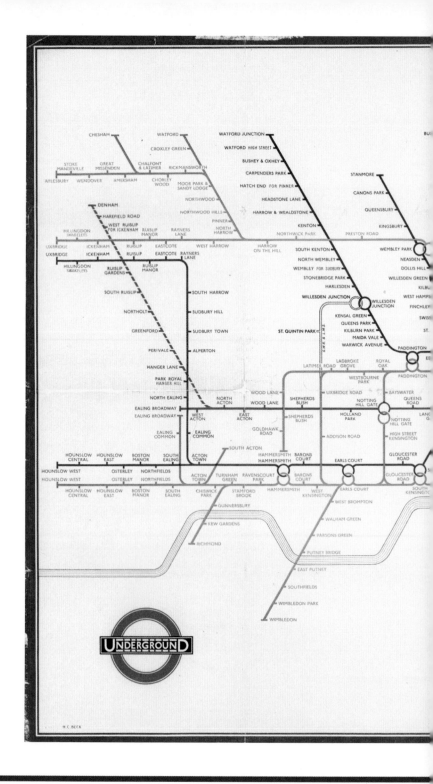

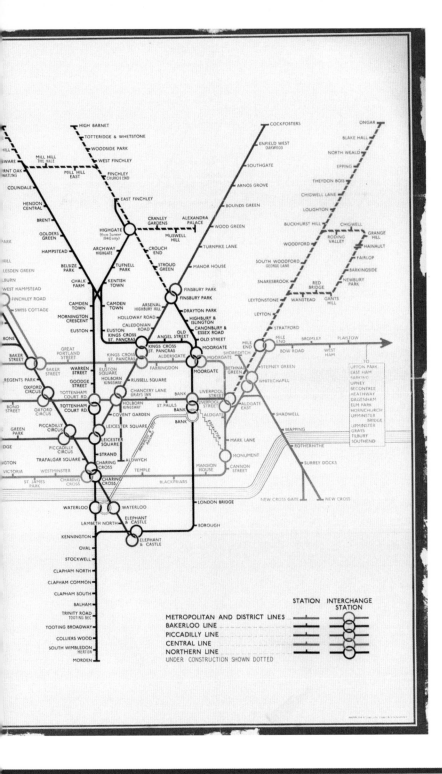

STATION   INTERCHANGE STATION

METROPOLITAN AND DISTRICT LINES
BAKERLOO LINE
PICCADILLY LINE
CENTRAL LINE
NORTHERN LINE
UNDER CONSTRUCTION SHOWN DOTTED

1940 Map: H. C. Beck

1. What piece of technology found most frequently in deep-level Tube stations features on this map?

2. Which two Underground lines, in operation in 1940, are represented by a single colour on this map? What Tube line is drawn in this colour on modern maps?

3. Which station on this map, whose name begins with U, is no longer part of the London Underground network?

4. What is unusual about the representations of Euston and Camden Town stations on this map?

5. a. How many terminal stations are shown as currently under construction on this map?

   b. Of these planned terminals, how many are Tube terminals today?

6. Which section of track shown as under construction is now the Parkland Walk?

7. The station St Quintin Park, to the west of Willesden Junction, no longer exists. The section of railway track shown, however, is still in operation. What TfL line now runs along this section of track?

8. On this map, the names of interchange stations are included multiple times, once for each line involved in the interchange. The name Kings Cross St Pancras, for example, appears three times on this map, representing the three lines it is served by. Which interchange station is the exception to this rule, where fewer name labels are present than the number of lines in the interchange?

9. In what way do the angles used to represent some of the lines on the map differ from modern maps?

10. Compared to modern TfL maps, what is unusual on this map about the relative angles of the Earl's Court to Wimbledon stretch of the District line, and the Kennington to Morden stretch of the Northern line?

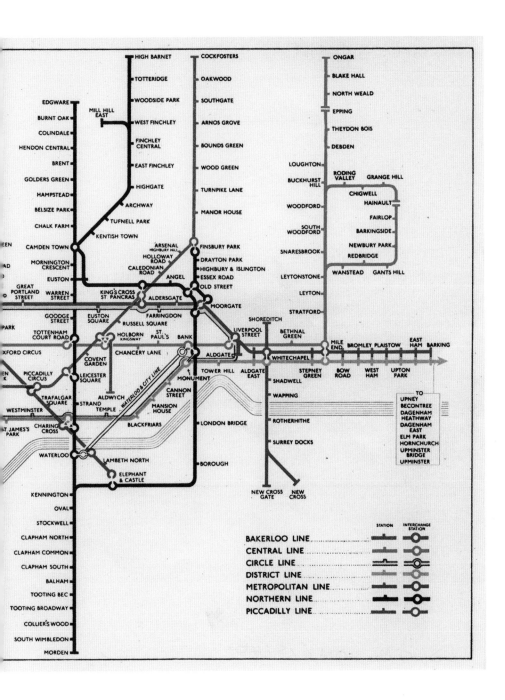

1951 Map: H. C. Beck

1. What is Aldersgate station on the Metropolitan line now known as?

2. Some station names have suffixes, either in brackets or smaller text beneath the station name. Can you find a station with the suffix 'Kingsway'? This suffix, now no longer in use, had been added in 1933, but to what did it refer?

3. Which station is the modern terminal of the Metropolitan line branch that ends at Aylesbury on this map?

4. How many of the Metropolitan line terminals shown on the map are still Metropolitan line terminal stations today?

5. And how many of the remaining Metropolitan line terminals shown are still terminals but only now on other lines?

6. Station names are printed on this map in black capital letters. Without checking, can you say how station names appear on standard modern TfL maps?

7. Which Underground line shown on this map first appeared on Tube maps in 1949, even though no new track had been built to create it?

8. The roundel in the bottom-left corner of the map features the name London Transport, which preceded Transport for London (TfL). What word appears within the roundel on modern versions of the same map?

9. Which stretch of track shown here on the Northern line is now no longer a London Underground line? What network is it now a part of?

1969 MAP:
Paul E. Garbutt

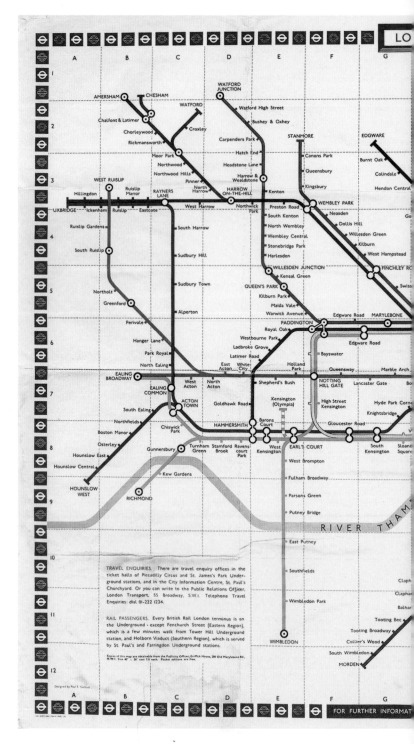

1969 Map: Paul E. Garbutt

1. This map indicates stations closed on Sundays with a red star. How many are there? Which one of these was closed permanently in 1981? And which one left the TfL network in 1975, but is still in use?

2. How many stations on the Northern line are interchange stations with British Rail connections, indicated by a black dot inside a white circle?

3. One of the stations in the answer to the previous question is no longer found on a modern Underground map because it merged with another station.

   a. Can you say which two stations these were?

   b. The two stations were given a new name, that was already in use on the map. What name was that?

   c. What was the existing station with that name renamed to?

   d. One of the stations in 'a' used a name that had previously been assigned to a different station shown on the map (although since closed) – which one?

4. One line on the map is shown as under construction. Has it since been built exactly as shown?

5. The Underground line identified in the previous question has only one station which is not an interchange station with any other railway line, as of 2020. Which station is it?

6. Which Piccadilly line terminal has since closed, and is no longer a station on the London Underground?

7. Which modern Underground line with terminals at Hammersmith and Barking is shown here as part of the Metropolitan line? It was not represented as a distinct line on the Tube map until 1990.

8. Which London Underground line now serves the stretch from Stanmore to St John's Wood, which is part of the Bakerloo line on this map?

9. Ignoring variations in shape and colour, what feature has the Thames gained on this map, which was absent from all the earlier historical maps shown?

Poster Puzzles

The following images are all original pieces of poster art, commissioned by TfL to advertise well-known tourist attractions in London, but with their original text cropped out. Can you work out which attraction is being advertised by each of the four posters?

1.

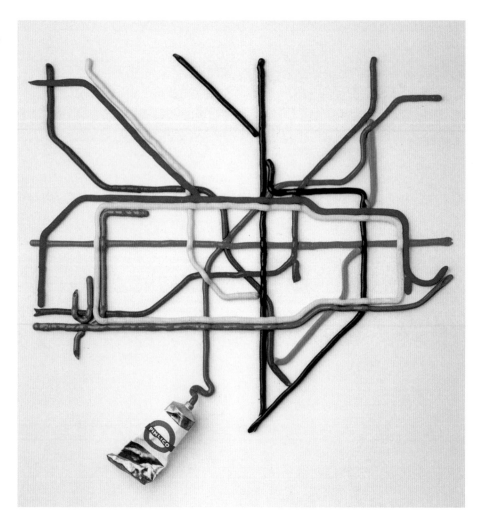

2.

3.

4.

Roundels

TfL's iconic roundel symbol has undergone many changes in shape, text and colour over the course of the public transport system's long history. Can you match each of the seven pieces of text below with the roundel design it belongs to? All the text has been converted to black so as to give less of a clue as to which roundel it is associated with.

The original roundels complete with text in the correct colours are shown in the solutions section.

1. HIDDEN LONDON

2. SHOREDITCH

3. VICTORIA LINE

4. TROLLEYBUS

5. BAKER STREET

6. EALING BROADWAY

7. LONDON GENERAL OMNIBUS

A.

B.

C.

D.

E.

F.

G.

Walking Puzzles

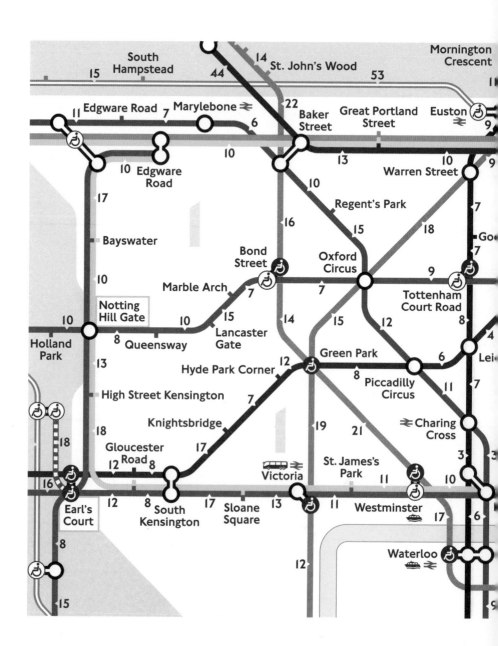

The map below shows the estimated walking time in minutes between certain stations. Answer the questions overleaf, assuming that you walk the route indicated by the times marked on the map.

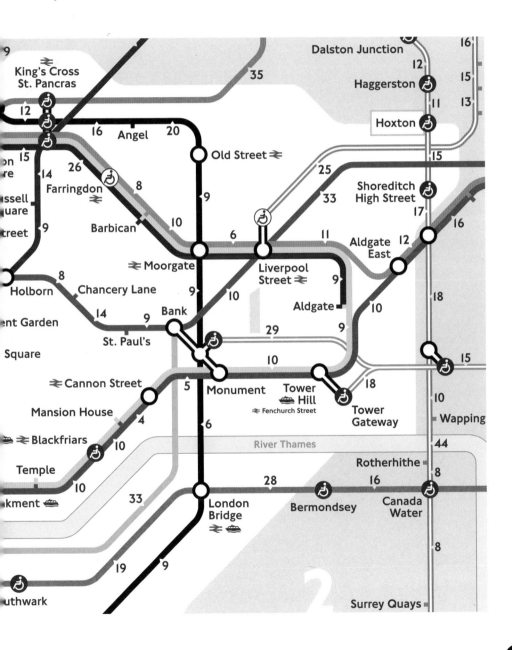

Walking Puzzles

1. According to the map, which two Underground stations are quickest to walk between?

2. Considering only the fully visible routes shown on the map, which two adjacent Underground stations on the same line would take the longest to walk between?

3. If you were to navigate from station to station using only the routes shown on the map, what is the shortest amount of time it would take you to walk from Warren Street to Liverpool Street?

4. If following these routes, would it be faster to walk from St. James's Park to Green Park via Victoria station or via Westminster station?

5. Is it faster to walk from King's Cross St. Pancras to Moorgate along the Northern line or the Metropolitan line?

6. And is it faster to walk from Waterloo to Baker Street along the Jubilee line or the Bakerloo line?

7. Which two stations ending in Gate are an 18-minute walk apart along the same line?

8. And which two stations ending in Square are a 21-minute walk apart along the same line?

Single-station Close-ups 7.

Can you identify the unlabelled station based on just the colours of the Underground lines shown?

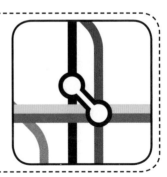

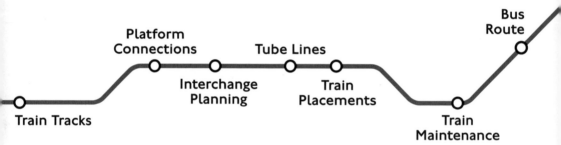

Train Tracks

Platform
Connections

Interchange
Planning

Tube Lines

Train
Placements

Train
Maintenance

Bus
Route

LOGIC PUZZLES

Train Tracks

Complete each train track, so the track travels from its entrance in the left column all the way to its exit in the bottom row. Numbers outside the grid reveal how many squares in that row or column contain a piece of track. In any square it visits the track may only turn 90 degrees or continue straight through. It cannot cross over itself.

1.

	1	3	2	4	4	2	5	5
2								
6	▦						▦	
3								
5				▦				
4								
1								
4					◠			
1		▦						

2. Only one additional track segment is given.

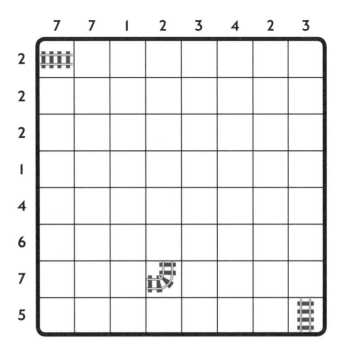

3. Rows and columns without numbers may contain any number of track pieces.

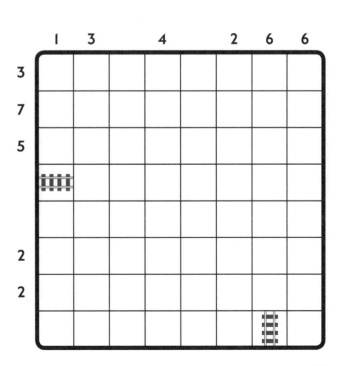

Platform Connections

Can you build the required bridges to complete each of these complex station layouts? Each circled platform contains a number revealing how many bridges must be drawn from it to other platforms. Additionally:

◆ Bridges must be placed horizontally or vertically
◆ There can be no more than two bridges between any given pair of platforms
◆ Bridges cannot cross over another bridge or a platform.

The finished layout must connect all platforms, so you can travel between any two platforms by following one or more bridges.

1.

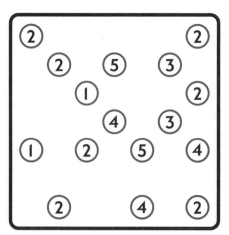

2.

3.

Interchange Planning

Join some of the dots in each puzzle to create a single loop of track. It must pass by the marked stations (indicated by numbers) on the given number of sides. For example, the loop should pass by a '3' station on 3 of its 4 sides, and should not pass by any sides of a '0' station. The loop can only travel horizontally or vertically between dots, and cannot visit any dot more than once (which also means it cannot cross over itself).

1.

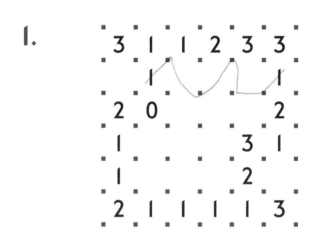

2.

```
   3     3 2 2   3
 3 1 2 2 3   1 2
   2   1   0 2 2
 1   3   3   3 1
 3 2   2   1   3
 2 3 2   1   2
 1 2   2 1 3 2 0
 3   2 3 1   0
```

3.

```
   1 2 2 2 2 3 3 2 3
     3 3 2   1 1   2
   0   1   1   1 3 1
 0 1   1 3   3     3
   2 2     2   1 1
   3 3   2     1 2
 1     1   2 2   2 0
 3 2 2   2   3   1
 2   1 2   3 0 1
 0 2 3 3 2 3 1 0 0
```

Tube Lines

Draw non-crossing train lines to join each pair of stations, indicated by matching numbers. The lines must travel horizontally and vertically between squares, and for safety reasons no more than one train line can enter any square.

1.

2.

1		2		3				
4							5	
	6		1		6			
				5				3
					2			
	7						7	
	8							8
								4

3.

	1	2	3					3	
									4
			4						
				5			5		
	1					6			
				7		2			
		8		6					
		9					8		
10		7					9	10	

Train Placements

Fill each of these train yards by writing a letter (representing a type of train) into every square, so that no letter repeats in any row or column. Also, two identical letters never touch – not even diagonally.

1. Place letters from A to F:

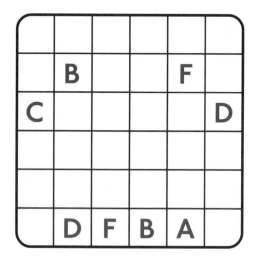

Logic Puzzles

2. Place letters from A to G:

			C			
		E		B		
	B				E	
C			A			D
	A				G	
		F		D		
			B			

3. Place letters from A to H:

		G	E	H	A		
E							F
A			D	B			G
D			H	G			C
C							A
		D	B	F	E		

Train Maintenance

Place trains into certain squares so that each maintenance depot, indicated by a circle, is servicing one train in a touching (but not diagonally touching) square. There may be more than one train adjacent to a depot, but if so then any additional trains must be being serviced by other depots. Each depot must be servicing only one train.

Numbers outside the grid reveal the total number of trains found in certain rows and columns of the grid. Other rows and columns can contain any number of trains, remembering that all trains must be attached to a depot.

For safety purposes, trains cannot ever be placed in touching – including diagonally touching – squares.

1.

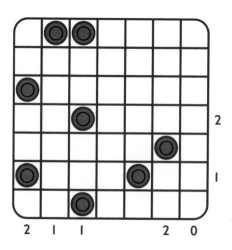

2.

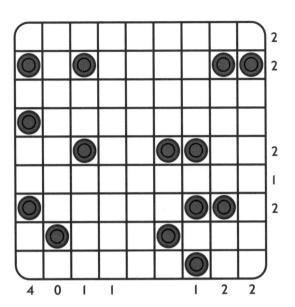

3.

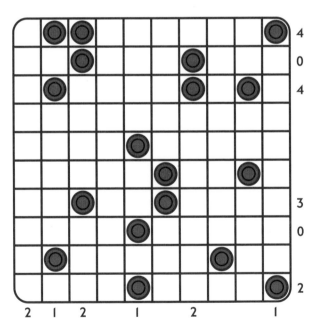

Bus Route

Draw a bus route loop, using only horizontal and vertical lines, that travels through certain empty squares to pass by every bus station. Bus stations are indicated by numbers, and specify the exact number of touching squares the loop must visit, including diagonally touching squares. The loop cannot enter any square more than once, nor any square containing a number.

1.

		5			
				8	
		7			
		7			5
	3				

2.

			5				
	7					8	
	7		7	7			
						8	
	8						
			5				

3.

	7	7		7			6		
2				8			5		
						7			
			8					7	
5					6				
								7	
			5						

Easy as TfL

Place the letters T, F and L once each into every row and column within the grid (not counting those given as clues outside the grid). This means that there will be one (in the first puzzle) or two (in the second and third puzzles) empty squares in each row and column. Letters at the end of certain rows and columns specify the closest letter to that clue, within the same row or column.

1.

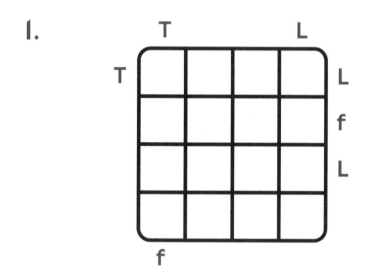

2.

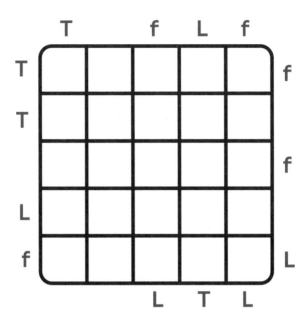

3.

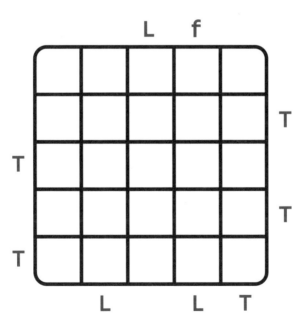

Train Yard

A complex fence is being put up around an unusually shaped train yard. Complete it by drawing a loop that visits every dot exactly once each, using only horizontal and vertical lines. Some parts of the fence are given already.

1.

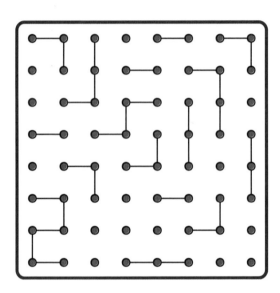

Single-station Close-ups 8.

Can you identify the unlabelled station based on just the colours of the Underground lines shown?

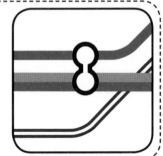

2.

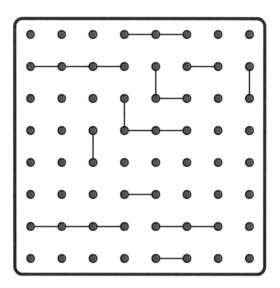

3.

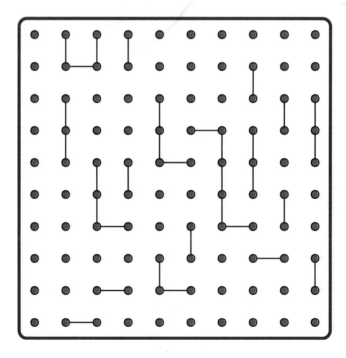

Bus-station Inspector

Inspect all of the buses that are parked in a grid, visiting them in the order of their bus route numbers. One bus is parked in every square, but not all of their route numbers have been marked on the grid. Given the range of bus numbers marked next to each grid, add in any numbers missing from the grid – one per empty square. You must be able to travel a route from the lowest to the highest bus number by moving only one square at a time from square to square, either left/right/up/down or diagonally, always increasing the bus number by exactly 1 at each step.

Example solution, using 1 to 16

15	14	13	1
7	16	12	2
8	6	11	3
9	10	5	4

1.

1–25

	17	16	25	
			22	23
12				
	7	4	5	2
9				1

2.

				31	
27			30		35
				36	
3		1	19		
		11	13		
	10				

3.

62	61						
64		60	58	48		45	
34		52			1		42
				39	40		
24							6
			30	29		8	
21		26					9
20		18	17				11

Local Journey

A stopping service needs to visit every single location that hasn't been shaded in in each puzzle. Draw a loop that visits each and every white square, but without visiting any square more than once. The loop can only travel horizontally or vertically between neighbouring squares.

1.

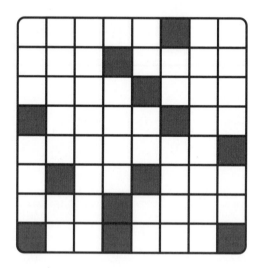

2.

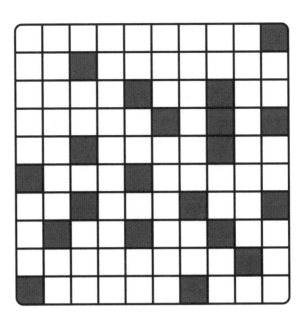

3.

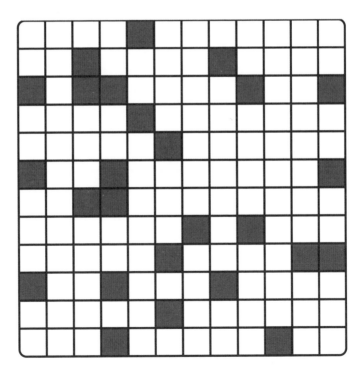

Cycle Route

Plan a cycling tour that visits every square on the grid. In each square the tour can either travel straight, turn 90 degrees, or cross over itself. Some of the tour is already given, and those squares cannot be changed.

1.

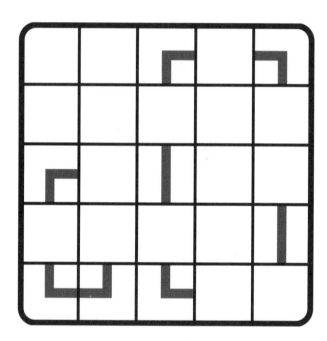

2.

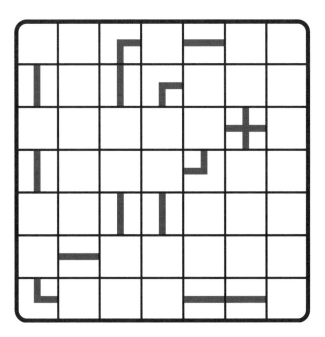

3.

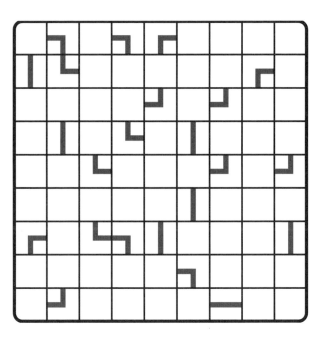

Wordoku

Place a letter in each empty square so that no letter repeats in any row, column or bold-lined box. When each puzzle is complete, a TfL-related word or location will be spelled out in the shaded diagonal from top to bottom.

Place the letters A, E, L, R, T and V:

1.

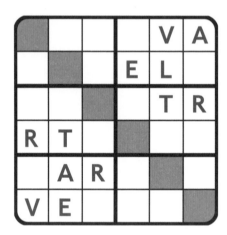

Single-station Close-ups 10.

Can you identify the unlabelled station based on just the colours of the Underground lines shown?

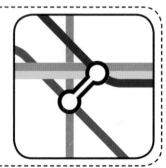

2.

Place the letters B, C, E, H, O, R, S, U and W:

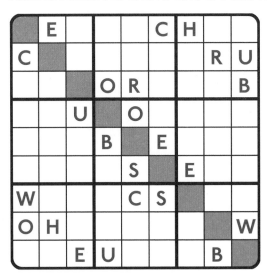

3.

Place the letters A, B, C, E, H, L, M, O, U, R, S and T:

		M	B						U		
U			H	T		O		E			
						E	C	R	H		
					O	B		A			U
		L	C		R					E	
	U	R				M	S				O
R		E	B					L	H		
	A				H		O	S			
T		M		U	S						
		A	R	H	B						
		B			C		S	L			T
		T						H	A		

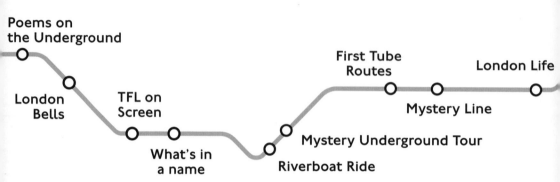

Poems on
the Underground

London
Bells

TFL on
Screen

What's in
a name

Riverboat Ride

Mystery Underground Tour

First Tube
Routes

Mystery Line

London Life

TRIVIA

Poems on the Underground

The lines in these poems by Oscar Wilde and William Wordsworth have been removed from their original positions and their order rearranged. Can you fill in the missing lines – listed below each poem – to reassemble the pieces? Some lines in each poem are shown in their correct places to help you.

I. Symphony in Yellow by Oscar Wilde

An omnibus across the bridge

_____

_____

_____

Big barges full of yellow hay

_____

_____

_____

The yellow leaves begin to fade

_____

_____

_____

- And, here and there, a passer-by
- Lies like a rod of rippled jade.
- And at my feet the pale green Thames
- And, like a yellow silken scarf,
- Crawls like a yellow butterfly,
- Shows like a little restless midge.
- The thick fog hangs along the quay.
- Are moored against the shadowy wharf,
- And flutter from the Temple elms,

Hint: the rhyme scheme for this poem is **ABBA CDDC EFFE**

2. Composed upon Westminster Bridge, September 3, 1802 by William Wordsworth

Earth has not anything to show more fair:

_____

_____

_____

The beauty of the morning; silent, bare,

_____

_____

_____

Never did sun more beautifully steep

_____

_____

_____

Dear God! the very houses seem asleep;

_____

Hint: the rhyme scheme for this poem is **ABBA ABBA CD CD CD**

- And all that mighty heart is lying still!
- Ships, towers, domes, theatres, and temples lie
- In his first splendour valley, rock or hill;
- Dull would he be of soul who could pass by
- The river glideth at his own sweet will:
- Ne'er saw I, never felt, a calm so deep!
- This City now doth like a garment wear
- All bright and glittering in the smokeless air.
- A sight so touching in its majesty:
- Open unto the fields, and to the sky;

London Bells

The locations in the poem London Bells, below, have been deleted and replaced with letters that correspond to the locations marked on the map below. Can you use your knowledge of London to replace each letter with its missing location?

Two sticks and an apple,
Ring the bells at WHITECHAP (A).

Old Father Bald Pate,
Ring the bells at Aldgate (B).

Maids in white aprons,
Ring the bells at _____ (C).

Oranges and Lemons,
Ring the bells at _____ (D).

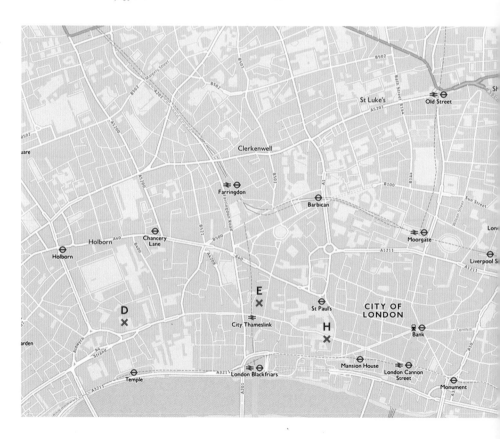

When will you pay me?
Ring the bells at the _____(E).

When I am rich,
Ring the bells at _____(F).

When will that be?
Ring the bells of _____(G).

When I am old,
Ring the great bell at _____(H).

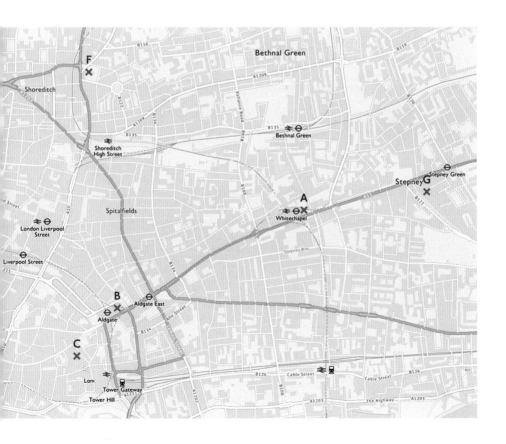

TfL on Screen – Real...

Can you name the combinations of films and TfL stations described below? The station names are all currently in use, although two are best-known for their mainline services.

1. An English-speaking bear arrives from Peru into a major London terminus, and adopts the name of this station as his own name.

FILM: _____

STATION: _____

2. A young wizard departs for his new school on a train leaving from this station in the first of a series of films based on books of the same name.

FILM: _____

STATION: _____

3. Two alternating storylines of one woman's life play out as she misses – and then does not miss – a train from this station.

FILM: _____

STATION: _____

4. A young tourist succumbs to lycanthropic wounds and sets out on a murderous rampage in London, including through this London Underground station.

FILM: _____

STATION: _____

5. A Norse god is transported to this station – and asks for directions to Greenwich – in an epic superhero film, the second in a series, named after its protagonist.

FILM: _____

STATION: _____

...and Fictional

Can you work out which films and TV series described below feature the given fictional Tube stations?

1. Crouch End station (not to be confused with the planned Crouch End Underground station, proposed as part of the Northern line extension to Alexandra Palace) is shown as being closed to the public in this film imagining a zombie takeover of London.

_____

2. Hickory Road station features in one episode of this long-running series following the investigation of a series of crimes by an iconic fictional detective.

_____

3. In one episode of this television series, an iconic detective is shown uncovering Sumatra Road as an abandoned station being used for nefarious anti-government purposes.

_____

4. Vauxhall Cross Underground station is used in this film as a secret MI6 facility with provisions for British spies.

_____

5. Residents of the fictional suburb of Walford are served by the Underground station Walford East in this long-running BBC television soap.

_____

What's in a Name?

Can you answer the following questions relating to the names of stations, lines, and other TfL assets?

1. Can you find two Underground station names that each contain every vowel?

2. Which current Underground station has six consecutive consonants in its name?

3. Which is the longest station name on the standard Tube map?

4. What is the most frequent word in Underground station names?

5. Which Underground station contains none of the letters of the word 'Underground'?

6. Which is the only Underground station to begin with a letter 'I'?

7. Which Underground line's name is a portmanteau of two of the stations it serves?

AT YOUR SERVICE

He does a difficult job with patience and understanding. He is one of 22,000 conductors who issue nearly ten million tickets to travellers on London Transport road vehicles every day.

8. What is the nickname generally given to the bicycles now operated by the Santander Cycles public hire scheme?

9. At the beginning of the 20th Century, by what nickname were the residential areas in north-west London served by the Metropolitan line known?

10. What is the current name of the London Underground line which, in the early stages of its development, was known as the Fleet line?

Riverboat Ride

Along the river below are clues to famous landmarks which can be seen from a tour of the River Thames in London. Knowing that the locations progress from west to east, can you use the clues and your geographical knowledge to work out which locations are being described?

Each landmark has four clues, but try to identify it using as few clues as possible.

1.
- Has a courtyard with an astronomical clock
- Currently owned by Queen Elizabeth II
- Holds an annual flower show
- Once the home of King Henry VIII

2.
- Has its own dedicated police force
- Is a UNESCO World Heritage Site
- Has one of the world's largest herbaria – a collection of preserved plants
- Home to a Grade I Listed glass structure known as the Palm House

3.
- Was built in two sections, known as 'A' and 'B'
- Is planned to be connected to the Northern line via a brand-new station
- Appeared on the cover of a Pink Floyd album in 1977
- Is famed for its four tall chimneys

4.
- Was completed in 1859
- Is officially named Elizabeth Tower
- Is part of the Palace of Westminster
- Has four large clock faces

5.
- Was designed in response to a competition to create a new landmark
- Is on the south bank of the River Thames
- Was the tallest of its kind when it opened in 2000
- Has been known as the Millennium Wheel

6.
- Work began on building a palace here in 1547
- Is the former home of the General Register Office
- Was once known as Denmark House
- Houses an outdoor ice rink in winter

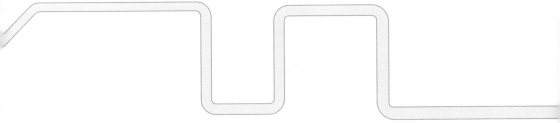

7.
- Was opened in stages between 1976 and 1977
- Is an example of Brutalist architecture
- Has a statue of Laurence Olivier outside
- Is home to three theatre spaces

8.
- Held the funeral for Admiral Nelson
- Is home to a Whispering Gallery
- Was rebuilt after the Great Fire of London
- Features a huge domed roof

9.
- The first structures here were mainly built of Kentish ragstone
- Has an entrance for doomed visitors brought in via barge
- At least six ravens ravens live here permanently
- Houses the Crown Jewels

Mystery Underground Tour

The following clues describe details of historical artefacts and design relics that can still be found today in certain stations along the Northern line. They are arranged in order from north to south, occasionally switching between east and west branches.

Can you follow the tour and work out which stations are being described? Once you've worked them out, you could also try looking out for them on a real-life journey.

- At this station designed by Charles Holden, a statue of an archer by Eric Aumonier sits on top of the entrance. It marks the final station situated above ground on the High Barnet Branch heading into central London. The archer has just fired an arrow – perhaps symbolizing the trains themselves – and is facing in the direction of Morden, the line's southern terminus.

- 'Heath Street' – the proposed name for this station on the Edgware branch – can still be seen on tiling on the platform walls. At 58m below ground, this station is the deepest on the London Underground network, relative to the ground level of its entrance.

- Like many other stations designed by Leslie Green, this Edgware branch station features iconic tiling. The outer facade features TfL's famous oxblood tiles, and is the longest frontage to do so, while the green dado tiles within feature a rare pomegranate motif. The building is now Grade II Listed.

- This station – whose name was originally proposed as Seymour Street – features unusual ironwork on its ventilation grilles for the lift shafts. Once commonplace in Leslie Green-designed stations, the grilles feature botanical elements designed in the Art Nouveau style.

- This stop can be accessed from Trafalgar Square, which once lent its name to this station. Along the length of the Northern line platform a huge black and white mural, designed by David Gentleman, depicts the construction of a memorial to Queen Eleanor of Castile. The name of the completed memorial – marking the final stop of her funeral cortege on its journey to Westminster – gives the station its name.

- The final station is one of only two remaining on the Underground network to feature an island platform, with both north and southbound trains accessed from a shared platform, in a deep-level tunnel. It also features an air-raid tunnel underneath the platforms and when it opened in 1900, the station became the new terminus of the City & South London Railway.

First Tube Routes

START AND END POINTS

As the Tube network has expanded over time, some line routes are now very different from when they first opened. In the puzzles below, the original start and end points of some Tube lines are given, albeit using their modern names, but have been altered to remove any letters found in the name of their line. In order to disguise them further still, the letters of another short word have also been removed, as shown for each question. Despite these changes, can you identify the old start and end points?

1. Line: DISTRICT;   Extra deleted word: GONE

   UH K ⟶ WM

2. Line: CENTRAL;   Extra deleted word: RUSH

   PD' B ⟶ BK

3. Line: BAKERLOO;   Extra deleted word: HILL

   STT ⟶ MT NT

THE METROPOLITAN LINE

In this puzzle, all of the modern-day stations which were on the original Metropolitan line are listed, with the letters of the word 'metropolitan' removed. Can you decipher the stations? Stations in bold had a different name when the line was formed.

DDG → DGW D → BK S → G D S → US SQU → KG'S CSS S CS → FGD

MYSTERY LINE

Which London Underground line is being described below?

Original Terminals: Stanmore to Charing Cross
Opened: 1st May 1979
Number of stations in 2019: 27
Line length in 2019: 36.2km

Trivia

Tube Lines Opening Dates

Can you draw lines to match these London Underground lines to the year in which they first opened?

Bonus Question: Which of these lines opened on Christmas Eve?

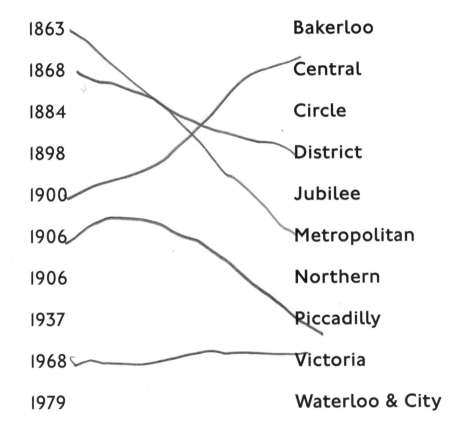

1863	Bakerloo
1868	Central
1884	Circle
1898	District
1900	Jubilee
1906	Metropolitan
1906	Northern
1937	Piccadilly
1968	Victoria
1979	Waterloo & City

Old vs New Station Names

Below is a list of the current and former names of certain Underground stations. Can you match the previous and current station names into their corresponding pairs?

1.

Acton Green   Chiswick Park

Brentford Road   Euston Square

Euston Road   Goodge Street

Gower Street   Gunnersbury

Great Central   Ladbroke Grove

Trinity Road   Marylebone

Notting Hill   Tooting Bec

Tottenham Court Road   Warren Street

2. Here are some further old names for Underground stations, presented cryptically as images which are given beneath their current names. Can you work out their original names, noting that pictures which are touching form part of the same word?

a. St Pauls:

b. Fulham Broadway:

c. Monument:

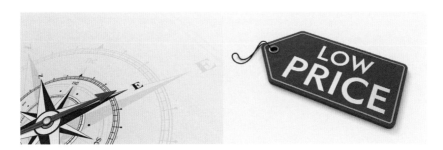

d. Acton Town:

London Life

1. All of the films in the table below are set (either wholly or partially) in London. Match each film with an actor who starred in it, using each actor and each film exactly once.

A Fish Called Wanda (1988)	Hugh Grant
Bridget Jones's Diary (2001)	Jamie Lee Curtis
The Iron Lady (2011)	Meryl Streep
Notting Hill (1999)	Pierce Brosnan
Shaun of the Dead (2004)	Renée Zellweger
Sherlock Holmes (2009)	Robert Downey Jr.
The World is Not Enough (1999)	Simon Pegg

2. Which hotel, famously associated with glitz and glamour, can be found on the opposite side of Piccadilly to the Royal Academy of Arts?

3. What do St Paul's Cathedral, the Old Royal Naval College, and the Royal Observatory have in common?

4. Which one of these four songs does not mention London or a London location?

- ◆ 'Common People', by Pulp
- ◆ 'You Can't Always Get What You Want', by The Rolling Stones,
- ◆ 'All the Young Dudes', by David Bowie
- ◆ 'LDN', by Lily Allen

5. Can you match each song about London with the artist who performed it?

'London Calling'	Bee Gees
'Streets of London'	Coldplay
'Violet Hill'	Dire Straits
'Walking Back to Waterloo'	Duffy
'Warwick Avenue'	Pet Shop Boys
'Waterloo Sunset'	Ralph McTell
'West End Girls'	The Clash
'Wild West End'	The Kinks

6. The following word fragments are the first and last names of six celebrities who were born in London (or are thought to have been born in London). They have been split up and the pieces arranged into alphabetical order. Can you rearrange the fragments and restore the names?

ALF	AN	CHA	CHA	CO
CK	EN	GA	GHT	HEL
HI	IN	KEI	KNI	LEY
MAN	MIR	NA	OLD	PL
RA	RED	REN	RLIE	RY
TCH	TOUR	WIN		

A to Z Quiz

Do you know your A to Z of TfL and London? Try these quiz questions, where each answer starts with a different letter of the alphabet in turn – so the answer to question A begins with an A, question B with B, and so on – except for X. If the answer is more than one word then only the first word is guaranteed to begin with the relevant letter.

A. Which Metropolitan line station beginning with 'A' is in Zone 9?

B. Which station takes its name from the occupants of a monastery which once stood near the modern site until 1538? Their name derived from a garment they habitually wore.

C. Near which appropriately named DLR stop can you find a vessel built to carry tea across the ocean?

For the Derby
Morden Station

thence by bus
every minute

SUMMER MEETING
30 May - 2 June

D. Statues of which prehistoric creatures can be found in Crystal Palace Park, near the Crystal Palace Overground station in south-east London?

E. Which Surrey town famed for its horse-racing is this poster advertising? The original name has been blurred out.

F. What name is given to the type of moulded glazed ceramic ware which can be found cladding many London Underground stations?

G. Which station beginning with 'G' would be a sensible place to exit for Buckingham Palace?

H. What is the name of the fare allowing unlimited bus and tram travel within one hour of first boarding, introduced in September 2016?

I. Which area of east London served by the DLR has a name apparently describing a location full of canines?

J. Which London Underground line has a map colour chosen to match with the event it is named after?

K. Which south-west London attraction is this poster advertising? The original name has been blurred out.

A Pageant of Flowers

By
UNDERGROUND

L. Which London terminal station shares the first part of its name with a city in Merseyside?

M. Which Underground station takes its name from the official home and office of the Lord Mayor of London?

N. Which area of London hosts a well-known carnival over the August bank holiday each year?

O. Which type of horse-drawn vehicle was introduced to London in 1829 by George Shillibeer, after he observed its success in Paris?

P. Which west-London bridge does the Oxford and Cambridge Boat Race start by?

Q. On the DLR line, 'Heron', 'South' and 'West India' all precede which word, or its plural?

R. Which is the largest of London's eight Royal Parks?

S. Which station is located on a junction with the same street as the Wimbledon Championships?

T. Which type of transport ran its last service in London in 1952, then began again with a new network in 2000?

U. Which station beginning with 'U' in the borough of Havering is a District line terminal?

V. Which Italian city lends its name to a 'Little' district in the area around the Regent's Canal?

W. What 'W' is the type of the thousands of boats that were once used to transport Londoners up and down the Thames, prior to steamboats and new bridges?

X. There are three Tube stations on the Victoria line which feature an 'X' somewhere in their name. Can you name them all?

Y. What is the official name of the ceremonial guardians of the Tower of London?

Z. Which word has been blurred out on this poster, which is advertising a major London attraction?

NOW HE'S AT THE

CAMDEN TOWN   CHALK FARM
OR ST JOHNS WOOD STATIONS

Solutions

WORD PUZZLES

MINI CODEWORDS

1.

C A N N O N   S T R E E T

D A G E N H A M   E A S T

M O O R G A T E

C H A N C E R Y   L A N E

V A U X H A L L

B A K E R   S T R E E T

1	2	3	4	5	6	7	8	9	10	11	12
S	R	D	E	G	C	T	Y	A	O	L	H

13	14	15	16	17	18	19
N	V	U	M	X	B	K

2.

K E N S A L   R I S E

W E S T   B R O M P T O N

I M P E R I A L   W H A R F

P E C K H A M   R Y E

C A N O N B U R Y

C A M D E N   R O A D

1	2	3	4	5	6	7	8	9	10	11	12
A	B	E	I	L	M	K	H	N	R	W	F

13	14	15	16	17	18	19	20
S	C	T	U	Y	O	D	P

3.

A L L   S A I N T S

E A S T   I N D I A

R O Y A L   V I C T O R I A

C Y P R U S

G A L L I O N S   R E A C H

B E C K T O N

1	2	3	4	5	6	7	8	9	10	11	12
E	I	P	R	V	G	A	N	U	O	D	L

13	14	15	16	17	18	19
C	T	S	B	Y	K	H

LETTER SOUP

Anytime

Oyster

Peak

Return

Single

STATION CONNECTIONS

I.

F I N S B U R Y   P A R K
E U S T O N
G R E E N   P A R K
V I C T O R I A
V A U X H A L L
B R I X T O N

2.

S T A N M O R E
M O R D E N
E P P I N G
U X B R I D G E
B R I X T O N
C O C K F O S T E R S

3.

W O O D   L A N E
M O O R G A T E
G O O D G E   S T R E E T
L I V E R P O O L   S T R E E T
W A R R E N   S T R E E T
F A R R I N G D O N

4.

S O U T H   K E N T O N
S T E P N E Y   G R E E N
S T O K E   N E W I N G T O N
S O U T H   W I M B L E D O N
S U D B U R Y   T O W N
S O U T H   A C T O N

WORD LADDERS

1. The two stations are Colliers Wood and East Putney, and the word ladder is completed as follows:

| WOOD |
| MOOD |
| MOOT |
| MOST |
| MAST |
| EAST |

Bonus question: To travel from one to the other with only one change on the Underground, you would have to travel from Colliers Wood on Northern line via Bank, then change at Monument to a District line train for Wimbledon. At peak times, you can also take the Northern line via Charing Cross and change at Embankment to a District line train to Wimbledon.

2. The two stations are Chalk Farm and Shepherd's Bush, and the word ladder is completed as shown:
    Bonus question: Both stations are in Zone 2.

| FARM |
| FARE |
| BARE |
| BASE |
| BASH |
| BUSH |

3. The two stations are
   Bank and Caledonian
   Road, and one way to
   complete the ladder is
   as shown to the right:
   Bonus question:
   The other London
   Underground station
   name consisting of only
   four letters is 'Oval'.

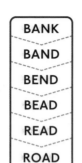

BANK
BAND
BEND
BEAD
READ
ROAD

3
a. Ahead
b. ETA (Estimated Time of Arrival)
c. Headway
d. Tea
e. Dagenham Heathway

4
a. Dial
b. Gadding
c. Toll
d. Lion
e. Addington Village

5. Rail Replacement Bus Service

LETTER TRIANGLES

The phrase is: 'STAND BEHIND THE
YELLOW LINE'

WORD SQUARES

1
a. Red
b. East
c. Star
d. Arena
e. Santander

2
a. Bat
b. Air
c. Oar
d. Via
e. Riverboat

CODEWORD

The highlighted words are **timetable**,
loco, **brakes** and **rails**. The circled letters
are an anagram of **Belsize Park**, found on
the Northern line.

WORD SEARCH: FINDING YOUR WAY

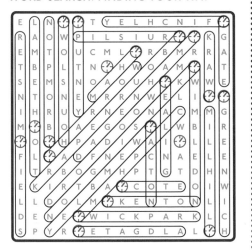

WORD SEARCH: MISSING THE BUS

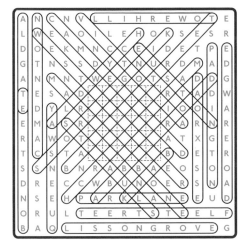

WORD CIRCLES

I.
a) Transport
b) Star (Lane)
c) Strap
d) Post (Office)
e) Ports
f) Parson

HIGHLIGHTED CROSSWORD

The word that can be anagrammed from the highlighted squares is **Metropolitan**.

2.
a) Bond (Street); Old (Street)
b) (Mile) End
c) (The Millennium) Dome
d) Wend
e) Mind (the Gap)
f) Wimbledon

TUBE-LINE CROSSWORD

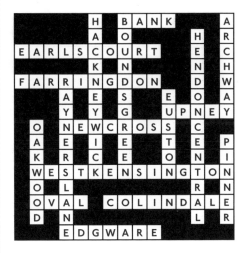

ZIG-ZAGS

1. ARSENAL
   ALDGATE
   TEMPLE
   LEYTONSTONE
   NEASDEN

2. CARPENDERS PARK
   PARK ROYAL
   ROYAL OAK
   OAKWOOD
   WOOD GREEN
   GREEN PARK

POSTER FITWORD

The grid had been rotated 90 degrees clockwise:

COMMON TERMINALS

1. BURY – Gunnersbury/Queensbury
2. TON – Kenton/Paddington
3. WAY – Fieldway/Archway
4. MINSTER – Westminster/Upminster
5. FORD – Woodford/Greenford

WORD SLIDER

1. BANK
2. PARK
3. BECK
4. LINK
5. PICK

CODE & CRYPTIC PUZZLES

ANAGRAMS

MILE END
WATERLOO
PADDINGTON
WESTMINSTER
LIVERPOOL STREET
NOTTING HILL GATE
SOUTH KENSINGTON
GREAT PORTLAND STREET

POETIC ANAGRAM EXTRAS

TURKEY STREET + C
KENSAL RISE + A
KEW GARDENS + N
HOMERTON + O
WEST HAMPSTEAD + N
WHITE HART LANE + B
CANADA WATER + U
SHADWELL + R
HEADSTONE LANE + Y
The extra letters spell out CANONBURY.

CODED QUOTES

Travel Quotes

1. Never go on trips with anyone you do not love
   – Ernest Hemingway
   Caesar Shift: +6 letters

2. The world is a book, and those who do not travel read only a page
   – Saint Augustine
   Caesar Shift: +3 letters

3. I travel for travel's sake
   – Robert Louis Stevenson
   Caesar Shift: +11 letters

4. Not all those who wander are lost
   – J. R. R. Tolkein
   Caesar Shift: +8 letters

5. Travel is fatal to prejudice, bigotry, and narrow-mindedness
   – Mark Twain
   Caesar Shift: +23 (or -3) letters

London Quotes

London is a roost for every bird
– Benjamin Disraeli

When a man is tired of London, he is tired of life
– Samuel Johnson

HIDDEN POSTERS

- dreams
- lusty side
- live
- me give

POEMS ON THE UNDERGROUND: FINISH THE VERSE

I know a garden in a street
Which no one ever knew;
I know a rose beyond the Thames,
Where flowers are pale and few.

CRYPTIC ROUTE PLANNER
1.
- Start at Golders Green (featuring two colours) on the Northern line
- Travel south past Chalk Farm (a place to mine bright white rock) to Warren Street (a rabbit's home road).
- Take the Victoria (monarch's) line to Green Park (a verdant recreation

POEMS ON THE UNDERGROUND: ANAGRAM ENDINGS
The end of each line should be, in order:
- streams
- tried
- Thames
- pride

ground), and change to the Piccadilly line (a darker blue than the Victoria line).

- Travel past Knightsbridge (armoured soldier's crossing) to Earl's Court (the quadrangle of an aristocrat – and it's the first one since there is Baron's Court further along)
- Change to the District line, which is green as per the word 'green' in Green Park and Golders Green
- Travel south past Fulham Broadway (the wide thoroughfare with a sliced meat, 'ham', in its name)
- Arrive at Wimbledon, where you might watch tennis.

2.
- Start at Redbridge on the Central line (which is marked in red) and travel to Stratford (the first part of Stratford-upon-Avon, Shakespeare's birthplace).
- Change to the London Overground and travel west to the interchange between Hackney Central and Hackney Downs (sharing part of their name with a hackney carriage – the official name for a taxi), and travel to Liverpool Street, where the line ends.
- Change to the Circle line (which is now a spiral, not a closed loop – and definitely not a circle) and travel west to Hammersmith (the dedicated toolmaker).
- Take a short walk to the District line (with its five possible terminals, not counting Kensington (Olympia)); take this eastbound to Victoria (a queen).
- Take the Victoria (queen's) line to King's Cross St Pancras (a queen's angry husband alongside a holy person)
- Change to the Metropolitan line (which shares its start with 'Metro', the popular name for the Parisian underground) and travel east to Liverpool Street (again).
- The route you have followed involved

taking lines in rainbow order: red, orange, yellow, green, (light) blue, magenta. Liverpool Street will also become a station on the Elizabeth line, which will be represented by a violet-like purple.

TWO WORDS, ONE WORD
1. Bayswater (bays + water)
2. Queensway (queen + sway)
3. Limehouse (lime + house)
4. Mudchute (mud + chute)
5. Clapton (clap + ton)
6. Stockwell (stock + well)
7. Moorgate (moor + gate)
8. Whitechapel (white + chapel)

LINK WORDS
WAY: RAILWAY and WAYSIDE
TRACK: SIDETRACK and TRACKLIST
ROAD: INROAD and ROADBLOCK
BUS: BATTLEBUS and BUSBY
CAR: TRAMCAR and CARNATION
GUARD: VANGUARD and GUARDANT

CONNECTING CLUES
I.
a. Bank
b. Oval
c. Angel
d. Archway
e. Embankment
f. Waterloo
   Connection: The answers are all single-word stations on the Northern line.
2.
a. Poplar
b. East India
c. Cyprus
d. King George V
e. Abbey Road
f. Royal Albert
   Connection: The answers are all stations on the DLR.

3.
   a. Drury Lane
   b. Trafalgar Square
   c. Piccadilly Circus
   d. The Oaks
   e. Warwick Avenue
   Connection: The above are all stops on the Number 6 bus route from Willesden Bus Garage to Aldwych

HIDDEN WORDS

1. Harlesden – <u>Charles, Den</u>nis and Simon all took the Bakerloo line to Charing Cross.
2. Bushey – 'Stop the <u>bus!', he y</u>elled, when he realized he'd gone past the stop for the Overground
3. Epping – Always take care when st<u>epping</u> from the Central line onto the platform.
4. Temple – If you need to report a lost or stolen <u>item, ple</u>ase contact a member of District line staff.
5. Euston – Victoria helpfully offered to sit alongsid<u>e us to n</u>avigate the journey more smoothly.

INITIALS ONLY

Great Expectations by Charles Dickens
Mrs Dalloway by Virginia Woolf
The Adventures of Sherlock Holmes by Arthur Conan Doyle
The Picture of Dorian Gray by Oscar Wilde
Strange Case of Dr Jekyll and Mr Hyde by Robert Louis Stevenson (sometimes the title is prefixed by 'The', but original editions omitted it)

MERGED STATIONS

OXFORD CIRCUS/WARREN STREET
(Victoria line)
PARSONS GREEN/MANSION HOUSE
(District line)
STRATFORD/SOUTHWARK (Jubilee line)
SHEPHERD'S BUSH/LANCASTER GATE
(Central line)

PADDINGTON/MARYLEBONE
(Bakerloo line)
KENNINGTON/EMBANKMENT
(Northern line)

LETTER PAIRS

1. BAKERLOO
   NORTHERN
   JUBILEE
   METROPOLITAN
   CENTRAL
   DISTRICT

2. ROLLING STOCK
   TROLLEYBUS
   ROUTEMASTER
   HACKNEY CARRIAGE
   VARIOBAHN
   LEYLAND TITAN

EVERY OTHER LETTER REMOVED

1. LIVERPOOL STREET
   BOND STREET
   LEICESTER SQUARE
   MARYLEBONE
   KING'S CROSS (appears as King's Cross St Pancras on the Tube map)

   Bonus Question: They are all squares on a British Monopoly board. Liverpool Street, Marylebone and King's Cross all appear with the word 'Station' following them. Additionally, these five stations can all be found in Fare Zone 1.

2. UNDERGROUND
   OYSTER CARD
   DOCKLANDS LIGHT RAILWAY
   FARE ZONE
   INTERCHANGE
   Bonus Question: The Docklands Light Railway, commonly known as the DLR, began operation in 1987

WORD FRAGMENTS

1. RUSSELL SQUARE
   CANNON STREET
   SWISS COTTAGE
   WILLESDEN GREEN
   NOTTING HILL GATE
2. MIND THE GAP
   STAND ON THE RIGHT
   WAY OUT
   PRIORITY SEAT
   SERVICE INFORMATION

SEMAPHORE

1. KEEPS LONDON GOING
2. THE WAY FOR ALL
3. IT IS COOLER DOWN BELOW
4. AT YOUR SERVICE

CODED SETS

1. The first letters in each block spell out the first station, the second letters the second station, and so on.
   The stations are therefore:
   BETHNAL GREEN
   SILVER STREET
   WANSTEAD PARK
   WEST BROMPTON
2. Consecutive letter pairs within the names have been switched, and then the resulting name has been reversed.
   The stations are therefore:
   BROMPTON ROAD
   DOWN STREET
   SOUTH KENTISH TOWN
   BRITISH MUSEUM
   KING WILLIAM STREET

MISSING VOWELS

1. ALDWYCH
   EDGWARE
   EUSTON
   UXBRIDGE
   ORPINGTON
   WILLESDEN BUS GARAGE

2. OAKWOOD – Tube station
   COVENT GARDEN – Tube station and home of the London Transport Museum
   LONDON TRAMS – Overground transport
   EMBANKMENT – London Riverboat pier
   ROLLING STOCK – Railway vehicle
   ROUTEMASTER – Bus model
   VICTORIA – Tube line and station

VISUAL STATIONS

1. Oval
2. Royal Oak
3. Waterloo
4. Finsbury Park ('Fins' 'berry')
5. Kennington ('Ken' in 'ton')

VISUAL PUZZLES

MISSING MAP

1.
A. Moorgate
B. Bank
C. Cannon Street
D. Monument
E. Tower Hill
F. Tower Gateway
G. Aldgate
H. Aldgate East
I. Liverpool Street
   + Bank and Monument were linked in 1933
   + Bank was the original terminal of the Central line
2.
A. Waterloo

3.
A. King's Cross St Pancras

4.
A. Edgware Road
   + The Roman road was Watling Street

5.
A. Chalk Farm
B. Camden Road
C. Camden Town
D. Mornington Crescent
♦ Camden Town had the proposed name
  Camden Road before it opened

6.
A. Oval
B. Kennington
C. Clapham High Street
D. Stockwell
E. Clapham North
♦ Stockwell was the original terminal of
  the City & South London Railway
♦ Kennington has the track loop

7.
A. Wimbledon Park
B. Wimbledon
♦ 2000

8.
A. Surrey Quays
B. New Cross
C. New Cross Gate
♦ Surrey Quays is named after the county
  of Surrey

DISGUISED LINES
1. Victoria line
2. District line

MOQUETTES
1. Barman – H
2. Green line – G
3. BEA (British European Airways) – C
4. Straub – D
5. Metropolitan Diamonds – A
6. Central line Check – F
7. Café – E
8. Overground – I
9. Elizabeth line – B

SPOT THE DIFFERENCE
1.

2.

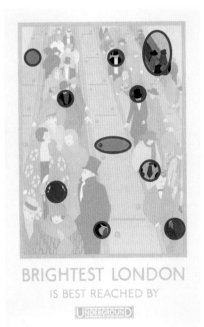

HISTORICAL MAPS
1925 Map

1. The station 'British Museum' can be found on the Central London Railway on this map, now the Central line. Built to serve the museum, the station eventually closed in 1933 after the expansion of nearby Holborn.
2. Mornington Crescent is shown here on the right branch of the two branches of track between Euston and Camden Town, whereas modern TfL maps have it on the left branch. This map from 1925 is the more geographically accurate.
3. The Hampstead and Highgate line, and the City and South London Railway form what is now known as the Northern line. The line marked 'Metropolitan Railway (Great Northern and City Section)' on this map was also temporarily included in the Northern line network, though it now serves main line services and does not appear on modern Tube maps.
4. They both feature small labelling lines linking their names to their station's position on the lines which serve them. The lack of space in the area showing central London means that these station names may have been confused with stations marked in close proximity on other lines, such as Russell Square and Regents Park.
5. Dover Street and Down Street.
6. Down Street, now disused, was used by Winston Churchill and his War Cabinet as a bunker during the Second World War.
7. Dover Street station is now known as Green Park.
8. Red, and brown. The line shown in orange is the 'Central London Railway', now the Central line, which is shown in red on modern TfL maps. The line

shown in red is the 'Bakerloo line (and L.M. & S.R.)', now the Bakerloo line, which is shown in brown on modern TfL maps.
9. The River Thames has not been included on this map.
10. Nightingale Lane. The station was renamed Clapham South for its opening in 1926 – the year after this map was made.
11. A small linear projection, the same colour as the line serving it, is used to indicate a non-interchange station on modern TfL maps.

1933 Map

1. Marlborough Road (shown on the map as 'Marlboro Road') and St John's Wood were closed, and a new St John's Wood station was opened. It is now on the Jubilee line.
2. The 'Morden-Edgware line'.
3. Post Office. It can be found to the left of Bank on this map.
4. Arsenal. The name appears in this map as Arsenal (Highbury Hill).
5. The Waterloo & City line.
6. Four: Ealing Broadway, Richmond, Wimbledon and Addison Road (now Kensington Olympia). The other three shown on the map, Hounslow West, South Acton, and High Street Kensington, are no longer terminals.
7.

   a. Hammersmith. It is the only station shown with three interchange diamonds, one each for the District, Piccadilly and Metropolitan lines. In fact, three other stations on this map are also served by three Underground lines – Charing Cross, Moorgate and Kings Cross St Pancras. Charing Cross is shown with only one diamond, and the others with two.

b. Interchange stations are represented by a circle on modern Tube maps

c. Diamonds can be found in the Johnston typeface used by TfL for all lettering. They are used in place of any round dots, such as in lower case i and j letters, in colons and in full stops.

1940 Map

1. An escalator. It is shown between Bank and Monument, where an escalator opened to link the two stations in 1933.

2. The District and Metropolitan lines are – unusually – drawn as one network on this map, printed in green. Green denotes the District line on modern Tube maps, although a lighter lime green represents the Tramlink network.

3. Uxbridge Road. The London Overground station Shepherd's Bush is now in operation very near the original Uxbridge Road site.

4. Neither are explicitly shown to be interchange stations, although passengers were able to change between branches of the Northern line at both of these stations. Both earlier and later Underground maps, including modern TfL maps, explicitly show them as interchange stations. Interestingly, the Northern line branches are shown as crossing north of Camden Town station, whereas they actually cross to the south of the station.

5.
a. Six – Denham, Hainault, Ongar (Central line), High Barnet, Alexandra Palace and Bushey Heath (Northern line).

b. One – High Barnet.

6. Alexandra Palace to Finsbury Park, via Highgate, on the Northern line. The track was built, but never added to the Northern line; it is now London's longest nature reserve.

7. The London Overground. This section of track was part of the West London line running from Willesden Junction to Clapham Junction, though many of the stations were closed in the mid-20th century due to falling passenger numbers and heavy damage sustained during the Second World War.

8. Waterloo, which only has two name labels, despite being served by three lines. Interestingly, Moorgate has three labels despite being served by only two named lines (the Northern and Metropolitan/District lines); this may be due to the Moorgate-Finsbury Park branch still being considered a separate line requiring an interchange station.

9. Diagonal lines are drawn at 60° angles, making them 15° 'steeper' than on modern TfL maps.

10. On modern TfL maps, the District line stretch is represented by a vertical line travelling down from central London, and the Northern line stretch by a diagonal line from right to left as it travels down from central London. On this map the angles are reversed, making the terminals of the two lines appear much further apart than they are geographically. In reality they are less than 1.5 miles apart.

1951 Map

1. Barbican. It was renamed in 1968.

2. Holborn – the suffix was the name of the road on which the station was located, although the station had been on Kingsway (and High Holborn) even before it was renamed.

3. Amersham. The Metropolitan line was only electrified as far as Amersham

after the end of steam locomotives, so it became the end of the line.

4. Four: Chesham, Watford, Uxbridge and Aldgate are still Metropolitan line terminals.

5. Three: Hammersmith is still a terminal, on the Circle and Hammersmith & City lines. New Cross is a terminal on the Overground, and Barking is a terminal on both the Overground and the Hammersmith & City lines.

6. On modern TfL maps, station names appear in dark blue, lower-case letters, with an initial capital letter for each word. (Occasional exceptions to this rule include 'Custom House for ExCel' and 'Cutty Sark for Maritime Greenwich'.)

7. The Circle line. It is shown on this map with a black outline, which is no longer used.

8. Underground.

9. The stretch of track from Moorgate to Finsbury Park is now part of the Great Northern railway line.

1969 Map

1. Nine. The stations are: Barbican, Blake Hall, Cannon Street, Chancery Lane, Covent Garden, Essex Road, Fairlop, Shadwell and Temple. Blake Hall has since closed, and Essex Road is now a National Rail station.

2. Ten: Kentish Town, Euston, King's Cross St Pancras, Highbury & Islington, Bank, London Bridge, Strand, Charing Cross, Waterloo and Balham.

3.
   a. Strand station merged with Trafalgar Square.
   b. They were renamed to Charing Cross station.
   c. The existing Charing Cross station was renamed to Embankment.

d. Aldwych station had been previously known as Strand. It has since closed.

4. Yes – the Victoria line's Victoria to Brixton stretch, shown on the map as 'Under Construction', opened in full in 1972.

5. Pimlico.

6. Aldwych. It closed in 1994.

7. The Hammersmith & City line.

8. The Jubilee line.

9. A name label, saying 'RIVER THAMES'. Two appear on the map.

POSTER PUZZLES

1. The Tate Britain Gallery
2. The London Museum (now closed)
3. The Natural History Museum (formerly The Museum of Natural History)
4. London Zoo

ROUNDELS

1. D

2. C

3. G

4. E

5. F

6. A

7. B

WALKING PUZZLES
1. 3 minutes between Charing Cross and Embankment is the shortest walking time shown.
2. 33 minutes between Waterloo and Bank/Monument is the longest time between Underground stations shown.
3. 65 minutes, walking via Goodge Street. If you went via King's Cross it would take 72 minutes.
4. It would be faster to walk via Victoria station at 30 minutes, whereas walking via Westminster would take 32 minutes.
5. The Metropolitan line is faster, at 44 minutes, as opposed to the Northern line at 45 minutes.
6. The Bakerloo line is faster, at 57 minutes, as opposed to 68 minutes for the Jubilee line.
7. Notting Hill Gate and Lancaster Gate, both on the Central line, are an 18-minute walk apart.
8. Russell Square and Leicester Square, both on the Piccadilly line, are a 21-minute walk apart.

LOGIC PUZZLES

TRAIN TRACKS

1.

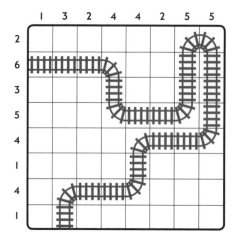

2.

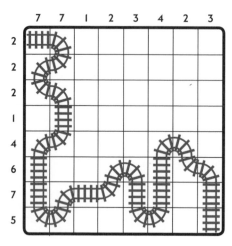

3.

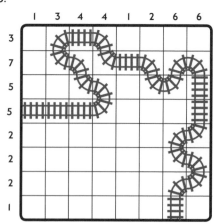

PLATFORM CONNECTIONS

1.

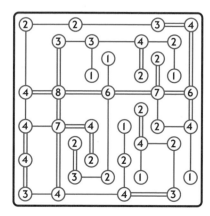

2.

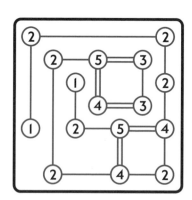

3.

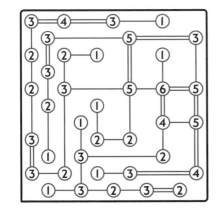

3.

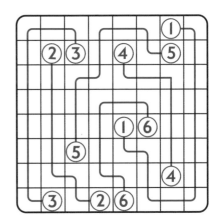

INTERCHANGE PLANNING

1.

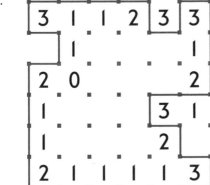

TUBE LINES

1.

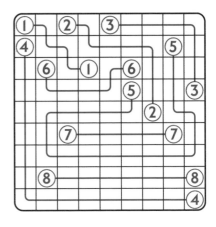

2.

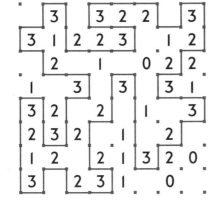

2.

3.

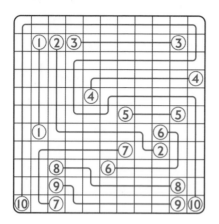

3.

F	D	G	E	H	A	C	B
H	A	F	C	D	B	G	E
E	B	H	G	A	C	D	F
A	F	C	D	B	H	E	G
D	E	A	H	G	F	B	C
C	G	B	F	E	D	H	A
B	H	E	A	C	G	F	D
G	C	D	B	F	E	A	H

TRAIN MAINTENANCE

1.

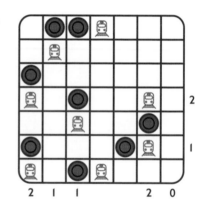

TRAIN PLACEMENTS

1.

F	C	E	A	D	B
A	B	D	C	F	E
C	F	A	E	B	D
D	E	B	F	C	A
B	A	C	D	E	F
E	D	F	B	A	C

2.

G	F	B	C	A	D	E
A	D	E	F	B	C	G
F	B	C	D	G	E	A
C	E	G	A	F	B	D
B	A	D	E	C	G	F
E	C	F	G	D	A	B
D	G	A	B	E	F	C

2.

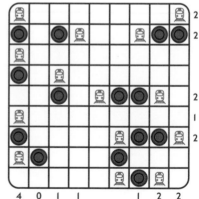

3.

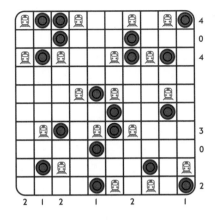

3.

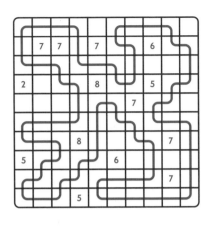

BUS ROUTE

1.

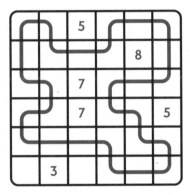

EASY AS TFL

1.

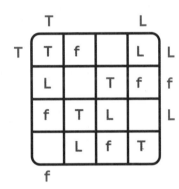

2.

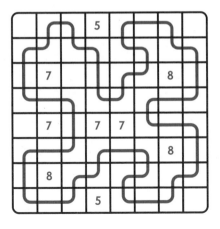

2.

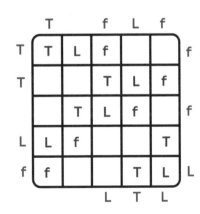

3.

	T		f	L
f		L	T	
T		T	L	f
L	f			T
T	T	L	f	

L   f

             T

             T

             T

L   L   T

TRAIN YARD

BUS-STATION INSPECTOR

3.

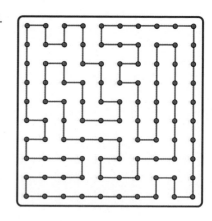

1.

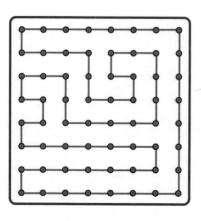

1.

14	17	16	25	24
13	15	18	22	23
12	11	19	20	21
10	7	4	5	2
9	8	6	3	1

2.

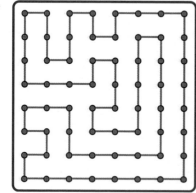

2.

26	25	24	23	31	32
27	28	22	30	33	35
4	2	29	21	36	34
3	5	1	19	20	17
6	8	11	13	18	16
7	10	9	12	14	15

3.

62	61	59	57	56	47	46	44
64	63	60	58	48	55	45	43
34	51	52	49	54	1	41	42
33	35	50	53	39	40	2	5
24	32	36	37	38	3	4	6
23	25	31	30	29	13	8	7
21	22	26	27	28	14	12	9
20	19	18	17	16	15	10	11

LOCAL JOURNEY

1.

2.

3.

CYCLE ROUTE

1.

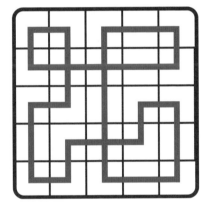

2.

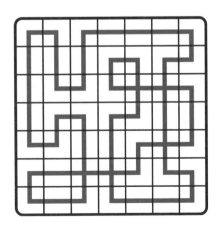

3.

WORDOKU

1.

T	L	E	R	V	A
A	R	V	E	L	T
E	V	A	L	T	R
R	T	L	V	A	E
L	A	R	T	E	V
V	E	T	A	R	L

The word spelled out is TRAVEL

2.

B	E	R	W	U	C	H	S	O
C	O	H	S	E	B	W	R	U
U	S	W	O	R	H	C	E	B
E	R	U	C	O	W	B	H	S
S	W	C	B	H	E	O	U	R
H	B	O	R	S	U	E	W	C
W	U	B	H	C	S	R	O	E
O	H	S	E	B	R	U	C	W
R	C	E	U	W	O	S	B	H

The word spelled out is BOW CHURCH
(DLR station, Stratford branch)

3.

C	E	M	B	R	S	L	H	T	U	O	A
U	R	S	H	T	A	O	B	C	E	M	L
L	T	O	A	U	M	E	C	R	H	S	B
H	M	E	S	L	O	B	T	A	C	R	U
O	B	L	C	S	R	U	A	M	T	E	H
A	U	R	T	E	H	C	M	S	B	L	O
R	S	C	E	B	T	A	O	U	L	H	M
B	A	U	L	M	E	H	R	O	S	T	C
T	O	H	M	C	U	S	L	B	R	A	E
M	L	A	R	H	B	T	U	E	O	C	S
E	H	B	O	A	C	R	S	L	M	U	T
S	C	T	U	O	L	M	E	H	A	B	R

The word spelled out is CROSSHARBOUR
(DLR station, Lewisham branch)

TRIVIA

POEMS ON THE UNDERGROUND

1.

An omnibus across the bridge
Crawls like a yellow butterfly,
And, here and there, a passer-by
Shows like a little restless midge.

Big barges full of yellow hay
Are moored against the shadowy wharf,
And, like a yellow silken scarf,
The thick fog hangs along the quay.

The yellow leaves begin to fade
And flutter from the Temple elms,
And at my feet the pale green Thames
Lies like a rod of rippled jade.

2.

Earth has not anything to show more
  fair:
Dull would he be of soul who could
  pass by
A sight so touching in its majesty:
This City now doth like a garment
  wear
The beauty of the morning; silent,
  bare,
Ships, towers, domes, theatres, and
  temples lie
Open unto the fields, and to the sky;
All bright and glittering in the
  smokeless air.
Never did sun more beautifully steep
In his first splendour valley, rock or
  hill;
Ne'er saw I, never felt, a calm so deep!
The river glideth at his own sweet will:
Dear God! the very houses seem
  asleep;
And all that mighty heart is lying still!

LONDON BELLS

A Whitechapel
B Aldgate
C St Catherine's (St Katherine's Cree)
D St Clement's (St Clement Danes)
E Old Bailey
F Fleetditch (St Leonard's Shoreditch)
G Stepney
H Paul's (St Paul's Cathedral)

TFL ON SCREEN – REAL

1. *Paddington* – Paddington
2. *Harry Potter* and the Philosopher's
   Stone – King's Cross
3. *Sliding Doors* – Embankment
4. *An American Werewolf in* London –
   Tottenham Court Road
5. *Thor: The Dark World* – Charing Cross

TFL ON SCREEN – FICTIONAL

1. *Shaun of the Dead*
2. *Agatha Christie's Poirot* – 'Hickory
   Dickory Dock'
3. *Sherlock* – 'The Empty Hearse'
4. *Die Another Day*, a James Bond film
5. *EastEnders*

WHAT'S IN A NAME?

1. Mansion House and South Ealing
2. Knightsbridge. When it was in use,
   Aldwych station would also have been
   correct
3. Cutty Sark for Maritime Greenwich – on
   the DLR
4. Park
5. Balham
6. Ickenham
7. Bakerloo – from Baker Street and
   Waterloo
8. Boris Bikes
9. Metroland
10. The Jubilee line

RIVERBOAT RIDE

The landmarks revealed on the journey
– travelling from west to east – are
below. Brackets indicate the name of
the nearest Riverboat station on the
Thames.

1. Hampton Court Palace (Hampton Court)
2. Kew Gardens (Kew)
3. Battersea Power station (Battersea
   Power station)
4. Big Ben (Westminster)
5. London Eye (London Eye)
6. Somerset House (Embankment)
7. National Theatre (Festival)
8. St Paul's Cathedral (Blackfriars)
9. Tower of London (Tower)

MYSTERY UNDERGROUND TOUR

From north to south (and reading down the page), the stations are:

- East Finchley
- Hampstead
- Chalk Farm
- Mornington Crescent
- Charing Cross
- Clapham Common

FIRST TUBE ROUTES

Start and End Points

1. South Kensington to Westminster
2. Shepherd's Bush to Bank
3. Baker Street to Lambeth North

The Metropolitan Line

PADDINGTON, EDGWARE ROAD, BAKER STREET, GREAT PORTLAND STREET (previously Portland Road), EUSTON SQUARE (previously Gower Street), KING'S CROSS ST PANCRAS (previously King's Cross), FARRINGDON (previously Farringdon Street)

Mystery Line

Jubilee line

TUBE LINES OPENING DATES

The London Underground lines opened in the order shown below, with the oldest first:

1863	Metropolitan
1868	District
1884	Circle
1898	Waterloo & City
1900	Central
1906	Bakerloo

1906	Piccadilly
1937	Northern (although parts of the route were in operation as the City and South London Railway in 1890)
1968	Victoria
1979	Jubilee

Bonus question: The District line was opened on Christmas Eve, 1868

OLD VS NEW STATION NAMES

1.

Acton Green	Chiswick Park
Brentford Road	Gunnersbury
Euston Road	Warren Street
Gower Street	Euston Square
Great Central	Marylebone
Notting Hill	Ladbroke Grove
Tottenham Court Road	Goodge Street
Trinity Road	Tooting Bec

2.

a. St Pauls – Post Office
b. Fulham Broadway – Walham Green
c. Monument – Eastcheap
d. Acton Town – Mill Hill Park

LONDON LIFE

1.

A Fish Called Wanda (1988) Jamie Lee Curtis

Bridget Jones's Diary (2001) Renée Zellweger

The Iron Lady (2011) Meryl Streep

Notting Hill (1999) Hugh Grant

Shaun of the Dead (2004) Simon Pegg

Sherlock Holmes (2009) Robert Downey Jr.

The World is Not Enough (1999) Pierce Brosnan

2. The Ritz

3. They were all designed by Sir
   Christopher Wren

4. 'All the Young Dudes', by David Bowie

5.
London Calling   The Clash
Streets of London   Ralph McTell
Violet Hill   Coldplay
Walking Back to Waterloo   Bee Gees
Warwick Avenue   Duffy
Waterloo Sunset   The Kinks
West End Girls   Pet Shop Boys
Wild West End   Dire Straits

6.
   ALFRED HITCHCOCK
   ANNA WINTOUR
   CHARLIE CHAPLIN
   GARY OLDMAN
   HELEN MIRREN
   KEIRA KNIGHTLEY

A TO Z QUIZ

A. Amersham
B. Blackfriars
C. Cutty Sark for Maritime Greenwich
D. Dinosaurs
E. Epsom

F. Faience
G. Green Park
H. Hopper
I. Isle of Dogs
J. Jubilee
   – after
   Elizabeth II's
   Silver Jubilee
K. Kew Gardens
L. Liverpool
   Street
M. Mansion
   House
N. Notting Hill
O. Omnibus
P. Putney
Q. Quay
R. Richmond Park
S. Southfields
T. Tram
U. Upminster
V. Venice, as in Little Venice
W. Wherry
X. Oxford Circus, Vauxhall and Brixton
Y. Yeoman Warders
Z. Zoo, as in London Zoo

KEW GARDENS
A Pageant of Flowers
By
UNDERGROUND

For the Derby
Morden Station

thence by bus
every minute

EPSOM
SUMMER MEETING
30 May - 2 June

NOW HE'S AT THE **ZOO**
CAMDEN TOWN   CHALK FARM
OR ST JOHNS WOOD STATIONS

SINGLE-STATION CLOSE-UPS

○

1. OXFORD CIRCUS

2. NOTTING HILL GATE

3. GREEN PARK

4. GLOUCESTER ROAD

5. WARREN STREET

6. HOLBORN

7. EMBANKMENT

8. MILE END

9. LONDON BRIDGE

10. BAKER STREET

1. Tottenham Court Road
2. Regents Park
3. Bayswater
4. Fulham Broadway
5. Whitechapel
6. Southwark
7. Preston Road
8. Chalk Farm
9. Hyde Park Corner
10. Warren Street
11. Bank
12. Chancery Lane
13. Waterloo
14. Latimer Road
15. Upney
16. Goldhawk Road
17. Canary Wharf
18. Pinner
19. Angel
20. Caledonian Road
21. Pimlico
22. Marble Arch
23. Lambeth North
24. Tower
25. Shoreditch

Notes

26 - Ladbroke Grove
27 - Kingsbury
28 - Great Portland Street
29 - Highgate
30 - South Ealing
31 - Seven Sisters
32 - Wanstead
33 - Maida Vale
34 - Euston Square
35 - East Putney
36 - East Ham
37 - Swiss Cottage
38 - Notchwood Cottage
39 - Balham
40 - Wood Green
41 - Victoria
42 - Holland Park
43 - Kenton
44 - Ruislip
45 - Bermuda
46 - Wood Lane
47 - Bermondsey
48 - Rickmansworth

49 - Golders Green
50 - Covent Garden
51 - Blackhorse Road
52 - Queensway
53 - Marylebone
54 - High Street Kensington
55 - Ravenscourt Park
56 - Stepney Green
57 - Neasden
58 - West Ham
59 - Mornington Crescent
60 - Bank Royal
61 - Hackney Wick
62 - East Acton
63 - Harlesden
64 - Gloucester Road
65 - Harlesden Road East
66 - ... East
67 - West Ham
68 - Hackney Wick
69 - Hampstead
70 - Manor House
71 - Chalk Farm House
72 - Bank Station
73 - Kilburn Park
74 - St ... Park
75 - Euston James Park
76 - ... Waterloo
77 - Ruislip Manor

79) Basize Park
80) Russell Square
81) Stockwell Square
82) Redbridge
83) Willesden
84) Sloane Square Knightbridge
85) Barking
86) Royal Oak
87) Canning Town
88) Liverpool Street
89) Oval
90) Knightsbridge
91) Brixton
92) Roding Valley
93) South Kensington
94) Paddington
95) Blackfriars
96) Hyde Park
97) Canons Park
98) Finchley Road
99) West Finchley
100) Turnpike Lane
101) Walthamstow Central
102) Shepherds Bush
103) Piccadilly Circus
104)

Notes